Finding and Confirming Truth

John S. Pletz

UNIVERSITY PRESS OF AMERICA,® INC.
Lanham • Boulder • New York • Toronto • Plymouth, UK

Copyright © 2010 by
University Press of America,® Inc.
4501 Forbes Boulevard
Suite 200
Lanham, Maryland 20706
UPA Acquisitions Department (301) 459-3366

Estover Road
Plymouth PL6 7PY
United Kingdom

All rights reserved
Printed in the United States of America
British Library Cataloging in Publication Information Available

Library of Congress Control Number: 2009943676
ISBN: 978-0-7618-5058-8 (paperback : alk. paper)
eISBN: 978-0-7618-5059-5

∞ ™ The paper used in this publication meets the minimum
requirements of American National Standard for Information
Sciences—Permanence of Paper for Printed Library Materials,
ANSI/NISO Z39.48-1992.

Contents

PART I. THE CONFIRMATION OF TRUTH   1

1   Is Confirmation Necessary?   3

2   The Means for Finding and Confirming Truth   8
     1. Present Perception   10
     2. Memory   12
     3. Reason   13
     4. Intuition   19
     5. External Authority   21
     6. Faith   22
     7. Intention   23

3   Confirming the Means   27
     1. Present Perception   27
     2. Memory   30
     3. Reason   31
     4. Intuition   41
     5. External Authority   42
     6. Faith   44
     7. Intention   45

4   Confirmation and Certainty   50
     1. The Accessibility of Absolute Certainty   50
     2. Degrees of Certainty and Assurance   62
     3. The Certainty Needed for the Confirmation of Truth   65

PART II. THE PROCESS OF FINDING AND CONFIRMING TRUTH — 69

5 The Steps Involved in Finding and Confirming Truth — 73
  1. Adopting an Attitude Conducive to the Search for Truth — 73
  2. Framing the Assertion To Be Considered — 73
  3. Identifying the Type of Assertion Which Is Being Considered — 74
  4. Selecting the Appropriate Types of Confirmation To Be Used — 74
  5. Applying the Appropriate Types of Confirmation — 82
  6. Weighing the Evidence to Determine Whether the Assertion Has Been Confirmed — 92
  7. Determining the Degree of Certainty to Ascribe to a Confirmed Assertion — 94
  8. Drawing a Conclusion about the Truth of the Assertion — 95
  9. Keeping an Open Mind for Future Evidence That May Later Have an Impact on That Truth Conclusion — 95

PART III. SO, WHAT IS TRUTH? — 97

6 The Basic Definition of "Truth" — 99

7 Using the Concept of Truth — 126

Index — 131

Part I

THE CONFIRMATION OF TRUTH

In order to know when we have found truth, we have to know what it is. However, this search for "the truth about truth" will not begin at the end (with precisely what "truth" should be considered to be), but rather with a discussion about how we can ascertain and confirm what that end may be so that we can know what we have (if anything) when we get there. Therefore, I will not begin this book with a survey or analysis of the definition of truth, but rather by considering how we might be able to know truth when we happen to see it-whatever it may ultimately be determined to be, exactly. Thus, while truth is the subject of this inquiry, the first order of business will be to review the manners in which we are able to determine when we may know that we have found the truth about anything-including truth itself.

While an extended discussion of the definition of truth would thus be premature, we nevertheless need to have at least some idea about what it is that is being sought. For a working definition of "truth," I will rely on dictionaries and their characterizations of what is sometimes referred to as "factual truth," which include "conformity with fact," "agreement with reality," "the real state of affairs," "accuracy of delineation or representation," and so on.[1]

How do we know when a statement is true–when it is "the real state of affairs" or when it provides "accuracy of delineation or representation"? There are two possible initial answers to this question: either we know truth because of something else–because of something other than the true statement which we consider along with the statement itself-or we do not need anything else in order to know it. I will begin with the second of these alternatives.

NOTE

1. See *The Oxford English Dictionary*, 2nd ed., J. A. Simpson and E. S. C. Weiner, eds. (Oxford: Clarendon Press, 1989), p. 627; and *Webster's Third New International Dictionary of the English Language Unabridged*, Philip Babcock Gove, ed. (Springfield, MA: Merriam-Webster, Inc., 1993), p. 2457.

Chapter One

Is Confirmation Necessary?

Some people believe that we know truth only because of itself-that we can distinguish between true and false statements through an automatic response or an immediate apprehension that we have of the truth of true statements when and as we consider them. Various explanations are given for our supposed capacity for doing this, including those provided by certain "intuitionists" (people who think that we intuit truth directly and that we need no other tool to measure the truth or falsehood of a statement). However, all of those who take the position that we know truth without the involvement of anything else-regardless of the reason why this would occur-believe that truth is self-evident and that the truth of an assertion becomes apparent when it is first thought, said, or heard.

Self-evidence would thus both cause and lead to the automatic recognition of truth. According to its proponents, this is as simple as recognizing the color blue. St. George Jackson Mivart wrote:

> The only ground of certainty which an ultimate and supremely certain judgment can possess is its self-evidence-its own manifest certainty in and by itself. All proof, or reasoning, must ultimately rest upon truths which carry with them their own evidence and do not, therefore, need proof.... Self-evidence is the criterion of truth.[1]

Aristotle characterized the indemonstrable premises of science as necessary, primary, and self-evident[2]; and the Stoics believed that there were "certain perceptions so distinct from all others and so *prima facie* true that no doubt was possible concerning them."[3] Baruch de Spinoza said that "The truth needs no sign" and that "Truth is its own criterion."[4] Ben Jonson wrote:

> Truth is the trial of itself
> And needs no other touch;
> And purer than the purest gold,
> Refine it ne'er so much.[5]

If truth is self-evident, then we should not need anything other than a given truth in order to know it. No external support or inference of any kind would be required for us to be able to ascertain when an assertion is true: its validity would simply be conveyed as it is presented.

A problem of self-contradiction exists here, however, because "self-evidence" proposes, on the one hand, that we do not need anything other than a true statement in order to know the truth of that statement, but then, on the other hand, it also asserts that its self-evidence serves as our means of knowing it. There is a difference between a true statement and its self-evidence, the latter of which only exists when we recognize it. Self-evidence thus becomes the test of truth: we recognize that a statement is true if and when it is self-evident to us. Because self-evidence serves as the means of knowing when we have a true statement, we are then using a test or standard separate and apart from the statement itself-one of the recognition of self-evidence–in order to provide inferential support for the truth of that statement. In other words, when we look to the attribute of "self-evidence" in order to confirm the truth of an assertion, we thereby become involved in confirmation by inference, as can be shown by the following syllogism which we would then be employing:

1. All assertions that appear to me to be self-evident are true;
2. Assertion A appears to me to be self-evident;
3. Therefore, Assertion A is true.

The argument that promotes or accepts the use of self-evidence as a means is simply not consistent with the position that we do not need anything other than the true statement itself to know that a statement is true, because we are then looking at self-evidence as the measure of the statement and as the criterion for determining its truth. The primary consequence of this is that if, whenever we try to apply the theoretical standard of self-evidence, we end up also using the test of self-evidence, we cannot then conclude that truth is known of and by itself.

Furthermore, when someone says that "Truth is self-evident" in this manner, what they usually mean is that they find a quality of obviousness in such statements and that a statement's truth can be recognized by that obviousness. That, however, is even more clearly a separate test: "All assertions which appear to be obvious are true; Assertion A appears to be obvious; therefore, Assertion A is true." While we may discuss self-evidence in the abstract as if it were some sort of instantaneous and self-sufficient knowledge, whenever we try to use it to distinguish between true and false statements, we normally are applying the test of our apprehension of its obviousness. And if we do that, we really are not acting any differently from people who employ other types of tests of truth: we are then just arguing about what may or may not be a correct means for us to use in order to do that.

The second problem with the position that we need nothing other than self-evidence in order to know a truth is that there really is no such thing as "*self*-evidence" in the sense of a statement whose truth is reliant *only* on its own evidence *by itself*. This is because no statement can be made in such pristine isolation. Consequently, self-evidence must always fail to live up to its name, because we can never accept any specific statement *entirely* on its own evidence alone.

Any search for truth has to begin from and within our current body of knowledge. We bring to any endeavor that involves thinking certain mental frameworks, tools, customs, and understandings; and we must use those as we apply ourselves to searches for answers to any questions which we may be addressing. No matter how hard we may try–and regardless of the lengths to which we may go in trying to "objectivize" it by divorcing our search for a specific truth from the existing mental frameworks and tools which are normally employed in the process-we cannot conduct this effort except through our normal mental operations using our prior understandings. Rather, we must always work within those "limitations." Therefore, even the most apparently true assertions are accepted because of and in the context of both the manners in which our minds work and the pool of knowledge which we already possess. As Brand Blanshard pointed out, even mathematical axioms and logical laws are not self-evident, but rather are bound up in the systems to which they belong.[6] Such things always constitute the presumptions and assumptions which we have and which we must use whenever we consider the truth of an assertion of any kind.

More specifically, every assertion has both internal and external antecedents. Internal antecedents include the meanings of the words which comprise the assertion and thereby become some of the unstated premises which are necessary to its meaning. For example, Rene Descartes' assertion of "*Cogito, ergo sum*" ("I think, therefore I am"[7]) contains, as internal antecedents, the meanings of an "I" (and the concept of a self), of thought and thinking, of being and existence, and of causation. Without those prior understandings, the assertion itself cannot be comprehended, much less perceived to be an "immediate truth." External antecedents are the systems and processes through which our minds operate and only through which an assertion may be understood and confirmed. The external-antecedent presumptions of every statement include the systems of language, logic, and memory which provide our mental capacities for forming and considering such assertions. Therefore, whenever we look closely at any statement which is purported to be true because of its "self-evidence," we can uncover underlying reasons why it cannot be true *in or of itself alone*. Rather, it can only be true in its context, as that is provided by its internal and external antecedents.

The third reason why self-evidence is an insufficient manner in which to find and confirm truth lies in its functional deficiencies. Self-evidence is simply an inadequate method for us to use in order to discriminate between the true and the false if it is employed solely by itself. As Arcesilaus said:

> When a wise man claims that he has such a perception, we call it the truth; and when a fool thinks he has one, we call it falsity. However, this begs the whole question, since we have no criterion for deciding who is a sage and who is a fool.[8]

Some people will tell us that "A is true" because to them it is "self-evident," and some others will tell us that "Not-A is true" because to them that statement is "self-evident." If self-evidence is a criterion of truth, then it is a most difficult-if not an impossible-one to use when we attempt to involve other people in a search to find the truth.

Self-evidence is also a functionally problematic means for finding truth even when we do not try to interact with others in the search. As Giambattista Vico said, when we stop searching for truth because we think we have found clarity and distinctness, we fail to put propositions to the tests that are necessary in order to see whether they measure up.[9] Each of us should also be able to recall times when we accepted as true statements which appeared to us at the time to be self-evident, only to subsequently discover that those statements were false despite our earlier confidence in them. When we are confronted with good reasons to believe that apparently self-evident statements are not really true (for example, the "obvious" conclusion that this table is completely solid when we learn about the nature of subatomic matter), then we no longer accept them as true. It follows that, if we are willing to accept, in appropriate circumstances, other types of inferences as proof of the falsity of apparently self-evident assertions, then we should accept them as valid means of supporting their truth, too.

While a strong feeling that an assertion is true "on its face" does provide *some* useful inferential support for the conclusion that it is indeed true (as will be discussed further below), the argument that an inquiry into the confirmation of truth need go no further than self-evidence is rebutted by its self-contradiction, by the recognition of the necessary antecedent knowledge and mental frameworks upon which each supposedly self-evident truth depends, and by its inability to provide a thoroughly reliable methodology for distinguishing between true and false statements. Because of these deficiencies in the self-evidence arguments, I believe that we must conclude that, in order to discern the truth of a true statement, we have to use something in addition to that statement itself.

NOTES

1. St. George Jackson Mivart, *On Truth: A Systematic Inquiry* (London: Kegan Paul, Trench & Co., 1889), pp. 10–11.

2. Aristotle, *Posterior Analytics*, 71b 9–25, Loeb Edition, Hugh Tredennick, trans. (Harvard University Press, 1960).

3. Phillip P. Hallie, "Arcesilaus," *The Encyclopedia of Philosophy*, Paul Edwards, ed. (New York: Macmillan Publishing Co., 1967), vol. 1, p. 145.

4. Thomas Carson Mark, *Spinoza's Theory of Truth* (Columbia University Press, 1972), p. 37.

5. Ben Jonson, "To the Author," *The Poetical Works of William Shakespeare and Ben Jonson* (Boston: Houghton, Mifflin and Co., 1879), p. 343.

6. Brand Blanshard, *The Nature of Thought* (London: George Allen & Unwin Ltd., 1939), vol. 2, pp. 312–329.

7. Rene Descartes, *A Discourse on Method* (New York: The Liberal Arts Press, 1956), p. 21.

8. Hallie, "Arcesilaus," p. 145.

9. Giambattista Vico, *The New Science of Giambattista Vico* (Oxford: Berg, 1989), p. 174.

Chapter Two

The Means for Finding and Confirming Truth

Confirmation is both the process of discovering the support which exists for determining whether a given assertion is true and the objective of that effort. The process involves the search for and the review of all of the known or knowable things which may either support or oppose the proposition that "The statement 'A is B' is true."[1]

We support or oppose the truth of an assertion, and thereby try to confirm its truth position (one way or another), by means of appropriate inferences. A valid inference produces a conclusion which has been correctly drawn from something that is already known. We make a valid inference when we accurately say, "Because of A, B," or "All A's are also B's; this X is an A; therefore, this X is also a B." Of course, many confirmations are far more complicated than that (e.g., "Because of A, B and C, and in spite of D and E [because of F and G], H"), and some of the inferential conclusions which we draw turn out to be incorrect. Errors occur when either the form or the content of a given inference is mistaken (or both); but neither of those potential problems undermines the effectiveness of valid inferences.

Truth-confirming inferences are those which can properly lead either to the conclusion, "Therefore, assertion 'A is B' is true" or to the conclusion, "Therefore, assertion 'A is B' is not true." The utility of the different types of truth-confirming inferences which we use is made possible by their major premises, which are derived from and rely upon different kinds of mental abilities or processes which can be appropriately used for these purposes. We employ these major premises because we have found that they can and do generate and support accurate conclusions about the truth both of specific assertions and of particular kinds of assertions. The major premises which we use in these truth inferences can all be put in the general form of "X is a valid method for us to use in the confirmation of truth." When one of these major premises is established as a starting point, we are then able to supply minor premises–roughly in the form of "I used X to try to confirm assertion 'A is B,' and it did"-and proceed to the conclusion, "Therefore, assertion 'A is B' is true."

The types of truth-confirming inferences which we may use are differentiated mainly by the foundations that exist for their major premises. To get to "Therefore, assertion 'A is B' is true," we must begin with an acceptable major premise which validly grounds the particular inferential process that we propose to use. We are then and thereby able to confirm the truth or falsity of particular assertions. For example, "Deductive reasoning is a valid way in which we can confirm the truth or falsity of at least some statements; assertion 'A is B' is the conclusion of valid deductive reasoning; therefore, assertion 'A is B' is true."

While drawing deductions in order to confirm truth as outlined above is itself a rational exercise, the different major premises which we may use rely not only on reason but also on several other sources which we have come to recognize and accept as being useful in this process. We routinely employ all of these different types of major premises in this manner (albeit not always consciously).

The idea that we use different sources and methods in finding and confirming truth is, of course, not new. Philosophers have long discussed differences between empirical and rational statements, for example, with empiricists finding truth in experience and rationalists finding it in reason. R. G. H. Siu described three sources of truth, including reason, intuition, and "no-knowledge" (his term for "ineffable enlightenment").[2] Pitirim Sorokin also listed three sources: sensate truth, dealing with the sensory aspects of the world; rational truth, which is obtained through logic, reason, and the scientific method; and ideational truth, which is super-rational and super-sensory and includes direct intuitions, revelations, and sudden enlightenment.[3]

I will use a different set of categories of the types of mental abilities and processes which we employ in these efforts because each one of them supports a unique major premise which we have found to be useful in the confirmation of truth. They include the following:

1. Present perception
2. Memory
3. Reason
4. Intuition
5. External authority
6. Faith
7. Intention

While some additional mental abilities have been said to function in the same manner (for example, extrasensory perception), they are not generally accepted as such, and I have no personal experience which supports their efficacy for these purposes. Consequently, I will focus exclusively on the seven sources of truth confirmation which are contained in this list.

A skeptical reaction to several of these suggested sources would be normal at this point, but I believe that it can be shown that each of them does provide some assistance to us in confirming certain kinds of statements. Clearly, these sources will diverge widely in their application and in their usefulness. When, however, we appropriately employ them in major premises (e.g., "Memory is a valid method for confirming the truth or falsity of assertions about something that occurred in my past"), and thus as beginning points for the determination of the truth or falsity of particular kinds of statements to which they may apply (e.g., to statements about the past, like "I remember eating breakfast yesterday morning"), we are able to confirm or deny-or to help to confirm or deny-the truth or falsity of the statements in question (e.g., "Therefore, it is true that I ate breakfast yesterday morning").

Which type of inference we may be able to use for which assertions will often depend upon the kind of statement that is under consideration. Different combinations of these inferential approaches will be more or less useful in confirming or disconfirming different kinds of assertions. When we use the right combination of confirmation tools which we have at our disposal for the consideration of any given assertion, we should be able to arrive at an appropriate conclusion about its truth or falsity–whether that is a clear confirmation, a clear disconfirmation, or neither of those (and thus an inconclusive outcome).

The rest of this chapter will be devoted to the presentation and consideration of the seven different types of major premises which can be used for the purpose of truth confirmation. Chapter 3 will scrutinize the justifications for their use and their effectiveness.

1. PRESENT PERCEPTION

Present perception is used as a means for the confirmation of truth because when we presently perceive something either through our senses or solely within our minds, we believe that what we are perceiving is really going on. If this is correct, then when I recognize that I am having such a perception, the truth of a statement asserting the existence of that particular perception is supported by a stated or implied inference along the following lines: "The recognition of present perception is a generally valid means of discerning and confirming them; at this time I perceive the sensation of a sweet taste; therefore, it is true that I am tasting something sweet."

Present perceptions are those things which we are perceiving *now*, whenever that "now" may be. The two major types of our present perceptions are those which pertain to our immediate internal world and those which pertain to our immediate external world. Internally, we perceive our mental states, conditions, and reactions primarily through an awareness of ourselves and of our thoughts and feelings. Externally, we perceive the physical and non-physical world which is beyond our own minds and bodies mostly through our senses.

While we are conscious, we continuously perceive–on some level-our present internal mental states. Often multiple lines of thoughts and feelings occur at the same time, because I may, for example, be feeling annoyed at one person at the same time that I am feeling pleased with another. We usually do not make a conscious note of the fact that we are having present mental perceptions: we merely process and act on them without specifically noticing them or focusing any attention on assertions which could be made about them. Most of the time when I am feeling happy, I simply enjoy that internal mental state; and when I am feeling sad, I lament how I feel, but I am not always conscious of the perception of my own internal mental state at that time-even though if I were to think about it at any time, I would recognize it. Occasionally, however, a thought or feeling becomes so strong that we are forced to expressly take note of it (for example, "I can't believe how angry I'm feeling, but I'm *really* mad!"). At other times we may notice our present thoughts or feelings simply by focusing upon them, either when we are by ourselves or when others bring them to our attention ("Hey, you're really mad, aren't you?").

Similarly, our physical senses (like sight or touch) receive continuous input through their particular forms of contact with the external world. While we have numerous sensations from our sensory receptors at every moment, most of them do not rise above the subconscious levels of our minds because we automatically filter out the unimportant ones (e.g., the sensations related to my sitting on this chair, unless it becomes uncomfortable) in order to avoid wasting our limited resources of consciousness upon them. Sensory assertions which do reach our conscious awareness usually do so because of their importance or because of their difference (which we may sometimes note with an accompanying "Ouch!" or "Wow!"), or because we intentionally raise them to primary awareness by concentrating on them. When that occurs, we convert our perceptions of those sensations from a passive to an active mode.

For both mental and sensory present perceptions, assertions exist or may be verbalized about them which are true. "I see that a light is on" is true if I am seeing a light that is on; and "I am relieved" is true if I am feeling relief.

With both types of assertions about our present perceptions, we can confirm them (to at least some extent) simply by our recognition of them. As C. I. Lewis said, "The simplest type of verification is 'observability at will,' wherein all conditions for verifying exist except my intent to make it."[4] This process begins with raw data (e.g., a feeling of anger or a sharp pressure at a point on my skin), but if they become important enough to us, they quickly are processed and recognized within the larger context which we provide based upon our experience and knowledge. We recognize that we are indeed angry at someone or that we have accidently stuck ourselves with a pin as we rapidly apply our mental faculties and knowledge to the perception. We continue to process the raw information being provided by our senses and through our consciousness until we are able to recognize its meaning and identify exactly what it is that we are sensing or perceiving. Thereafter, unless there is a specific reason to believe otherwise, we will conclude that the assertion (e.g., "The light is on") is true if we are indeed sensing or perceiving it (e.g., if we see what we call a light illuminating the surrounding area). And I will accept that it is true that "I am relieved" if I am currently aware of a feeling which I have come to identify as relief.

Our capacity for recognizing present perceptions thus provides the basis for a major premise which we use to determine the truth of assertions about such perceptions, which arrive–either explicitly or implicitly–at the conclusion, "Because I recognize this sensory or mental perception, my statement about it is true." It is, therefore, our primary means for confirming the truth or falsity of such assertions.

2. MEMORY

Memory is both a means we use to access knowledge which we have about the past and the aggregation of all of the specific bits and pieces of knowledge which we have about the past. The collective past impressions that we have constitute the content of our memories; but when we employ memory as a means, we possess the power to entertain in the present specific impressions about the past which have been stored within our minds.

The discussion of memory in philosophy has focused in part on its nature–on whether it involves something new which is occurring presently (which is known as the "representative" theory of memory, using a current image or an idea) or not (in which case we would be directly aware of our existing memories without the need for any such new representation). Philosophical discussions have also dealt with the problems that we have with memory, given its obvious fallibility, while recognizing its necessary role in all knowledge and for all assertions.[5]

When I attempt to confirm assertions about things which may have occurred to me before or assertions about things with which I may have had some other type of direct experience in the past, I utilize my personal memory. If I find that my recalled impressions coincide with an assertion that I am presently entertaining about something in the past-and regardless of whether it is something new or whether it is simply a direct awareness of that memory-then the truth of that assertion has thereby been supported. For example, the assertion, "I saw a bluebird yesterday," is supported if I can now recall having seen a bluebird yesterday. The confirming inference using memory may be characterized as: "My memory is a reliable source of true assertions about my past; therefore, because I remember X, it is true that X."

3. REASON

Confirmation by means of reason is the process of seeking and obtaining rational support for the truth of a given assertion. Rational verification has traditionally been the philosophically favored basis for truth inferences to such an extent that evidence produced through the application of reason has sometimes been considered to be the only type of proof which is acceptable for use in the search for factual truth.

Reason can be defined in the context of verification as the ability to recognize identities, similarities, and dissimilarities and then to conclude something meaningful about those relationships. Reason is also the mind's capacity to apply logic to steer us through arguments and evidence about relationships among objects and concepts in our world.

Logic is the rational activity of inferring from one or more assertions that another statement is true. In using logic, we rely on our two types of logical systems-deduction and induction. Because of their different orientations, each of them will be discussed separately.

a. Deductive Logic

Deductive reasoning is inference from a known or accepted assertion or assertions of a general nature that an unknown or unaccepted one must, necessarily, also be true. In its most basic form, from a general (or major) premise which has been accepted as being true, and a middle (or minor) premise connecting an individual case to the general premise, we deduce something about the individual case based upon the information provided by that first premise. For example, given the general (or major) premise that "Fire is dangerous" and the observation (or minor premise) that "This stick is on fire," we conclude by deductive inference that "Therefore, this burning stick is dangerous."

Deduction acts as the basis for this means of confirmation of truth in the same manner as do the other means which were previously discussed. We begin with the major premise that "Conclusions which have been reached through validly drawn deductions are true" and then proceed through a middle term (e.g., "Assertion 'A is B' is a correctly deduced conclusion") to the truth-conclusion (e.g., "Therefore, Assertion 'A is B' is true").

The process of deduction is, by definition, at least as old as rational human beings. For the earliest evidence of its formal description, however, we usually look to the works of the ancient Greek philosophers. Aristotle was the most important and prolific Greek writer on the subject; he was known for "the great reliability of his logical intuition."[6] Aristotle said that nothing should be judged true unless it might be made the conclusion of a perfect syllogism.[7] So central was he to the development of formal deductive logic that, until relatively recent times, Aristotle was not only considered to be its preeminent authority, but it was also around his work that the principal formulations and criticisms of deductive logic revolved. The so-called "Laws of Thought," which included the principles of identity (everything is what it is, or A is A), noncontradiction (A is not not-A), and excluded middle (everything is either A or not-A), could all be traced to Aristotle. While alternative deductive systems emerged, primarily in the twentieth century,[8] even those rest upon the fundamental concepts of deduction provided by its early proponents.

"Rationalism" is the term generally used to describe the approach to epistemology and truth which emphasizes the deductive side of reason. Rationalism's distinguishing feature is its abiding faith in deductive reason as the primary source and test of knowledge.

The roots of rationalism are embedded deeply in ancient Greek philosophy. Socrates and Plato accepted reason as the arbiter of truth and arrived at many of their conclusions through deductive arguments. Later, Augustine proposed the deductive principles of universality, necessity, and immutability as the "hallmarks of truth."[9] Medieval and classical rationalists also shared in the acceptance of deductive logic as the fundamental basis for truth. Rene Descartes was one of the most important classical rationalists. When he said that the test for judging the truth of the assertion, "*Cogito, ergo sum,*" was its "indubitability,"[10] the application of that test was accomplished through deductive logic:

(1) If I cannot doubt something, it must be true.
(2) I have tried, but I cannot doubt "*Cogito, ergo sum.*"
(3) Therefore, "*Cogito, ergo sum*" must be true.

Gottfried Leibniz wrote that "Truths of reason depend upon the laws of logic–identity, contradiction, and sufficient reason," while "truths of fact are established through the equivalence of definition . . . and the law of sufficient reason."[11] Immanuel Kant's philosophy was grounded in rationalism, although he also attempted to effect its synthesis with empiricism. While a number of later philosophers, like Georg Hegel and F. H. Bradley, may be called rationalists as well, those who are considered to be its foremost proponents lived centuries, if not millennia, ago.

Rationalism has produced a number of major tests for the deductive proof of truth. One of those is the "clear and distinct" test, which is related to the indubitability test. Two other rational tests of truth are derived from what have more often been discussed as theories of truth-pragmatism and coherence.

I will begin with the "clear and distinct" test. Clarity and distinctness are relational concepts, each one lying at one end of their respective continua, which run from clarity to murkiness and from distinctness to indistinctness. We understand neither of these concepts in isolation but rather as they bound their ranges. Consequently, we cannot identify a clear statement without knowledge about unclear ones, and we cannot know distinct ones without knowing indistinct ones. These are comparative judgments; Statement A is clearer than Statement B, but Statement C is the clearest of all. We operate most effectively in these areas by use of analogies. In this case, this usually involves measuring an assertion of unknown truth value against the "obviousness" which we associate with a known truth. Using a known truth as a prototype, the truth of the new assertion is allegedly confirmed if the latter's "clarity and distinctness" compare favorably with that of the prototype. As Spinoza said, "Once a person has a true idea, it can be used as a model for other ideas."[12] As a method, this test is applied deductively: "Proposition 'A is B,' which is clear and distinct, is true; another assertion will be true if it appears to be true as clearly and distinctly as does proposition 'A is B'; proposition 'X is Y' appears to be true as clearly and distinctly as does proposition 'A is B'; therefore, proposition 'X is Y' is true."

The pragmatic theory of truth has also provided what is essentially a rationalist test of truth. For pragmatists "a proposition is true insofar as it works or satisfies, working or satisfying being described variously by different exponents of the view."[13] William James argued that "The true and the satisfactory mean the same thing"[14] and that "Those thoughts are true which guide us to beneficial interaction with sensible particulars as they occur."[15] Under this approach, a conclusion is true if it results from the following kind of deduction:

(a) If an assertion is useful (or satisfying), it is true.
(b) The assertion 'X is Y' is useful (or satisfying).
(c) Therefore, assertion 'X is Y' is true.

The coherence theory asserts that proper verification of the truth of an assertion is found by determining whether it agrees or coincides with other assertions which are already known to be true. The coherence theory was advanced through a number of the great rationalist systems, including those of Spinoza, Berkeley, Hegel and Bradley.[16] But it has not been limited to Western philosophy: Mo Tzu, an early Chinese philosopher, said that a proposition's compatibility with the best of established conceptions was a test of truth.[17]

A relatively modern coherence exponent was Brand Blanshard, who explained its essence as follows:

> The degree of truth of a particular proposition is to be judged in the first instance by its coherence with experience as a whole, ultimately by its coherence with that further whole, all-comprehensive and fully articulated, in which thought can come to rest.[18]

Arthur Kenyon Rogers sought to justify coherence by arguing that it merely describes how we think and, therefore, that it must necessarily be accepted:

> Thinking is the bringing of our existing beliefs to bear upon the examination of a belief in particular; and the fuller the content of the experience interlaced in this apperceptive mass, the more valuable the judgment, though the precise nature of the elements present may not in the judgment itself be subject to analysis.[19]

Martin Johnson argued that the test for truth in physics is a test of coherence.[20] From another perspective, Teilhard de Chardin wrote that "The more I think about it, the less I can see any criterion for truth other than the establishment of a growing maximum of universal coherence."[21] Finally, the twentieth-century logician W. V. Quine wrote that "our statements about the external world face the tribunal of sense experiences not individually but as a corporate body."[22]

Those who accept the coherence theory see it as providing a practical means for determining whether a given assertion is true, and they justify it as a criterial theory principally because of its necessity, its accuracy in describing how we actually do go about verifying assertions, and its perceived rate of success. It is an ultimate consistency test, using the following as its major premise: "Assertions which cohere with a set of assertions known to be true are also true." The middle premise of the coherence inference occurs in the form of "The assertion 'X is Y' coheres with the set of statements 1 through 10, which are known to be true," leading to the conclusion, "'X is Y' is also true."

Deductive logic and its rationalist tests for truth provide significant manners in which we can verify assertions which may be true. The conclusions which we obtain through proper deductions, as well as conclusions which are drawn from the "clear and distinct" test, from pragmatic inferences, and from findings of coherence, are often of great significance in determining whether a given assertion is true.

b. Inductive Logic

Induction, which is reasoning from particular to general facts, is the other half of formal logic. When we reason inductively, we review a number of individual things and try to ascertain their similarities. If we find something about certain things in which they share, and if we have looked at enough of them to be satisfied that the same characteristic would be found in all like objects if only we took the time and trouble to review every one of them, then we are able to inductively conclude that it is true that the characteristic is shared by all of those like objects. Inductive conclusions can also be drawn about a characteristic or trait which occurs in a regular fraction or percentage of the group (e.g., one out of every ten cars around here is painted black).

C. S. Peirce explained induction as follows:

> Induction is where we generalize from a number of cases of which something is true, and infer that the same thing is true of a whole class. Or, where we find a certain thing to be true of a certain proportion of cases and infer that it is true of the same proportion of the whole class.[23]

For example, if all the snow that I have ever seen has been white, and if I have seen quite a lot of it and have no reason to believe that it could sometimes be of another color, when I conclude that "All snow is white," I have done so through inductive inference. Inductive conclusions are not *required* by their premises (I know of no reason why all snow would have to be white), but we find them to be rationally acceptable.

While inductive reasoning may also be as old as humans have been rational, the development of formal inductive analysis did not occur until long after similar rules had been produced for deductive logic. Francis Bacon, for example, was a pioneer in inductive thought as late as the seventeenth century. Inductive analyses have proliferated during the last 150 years, however, during which time tremendous advancements in inductive systems have been made.

Induction operates as truth confirmation by providing a major premise along the lines of the following: "Conclusions drawn through a correctly conducted inductive process are true, Assertion 'A is B' is a correctly drawn inductive conclusion, therefore, Assertion 'A is B' is true."

Because induction is most often applied to the external world, the inductive approach to verification is closely tied to empiricism, which argues that knowledge (or at least most of it) is obtained from experience. While formal empiricism, as opposed to rationalism, is a relatively recent development, nevertheless a number of ancient philosophers emphasized the importance of its principal tenets. Epicurus, for example, believed that the senses themselves never deceive us and that the whole superstructure of reason begins with the senses.[24] The major classical empiricists, however, were two eighteenth-century British philosophers, John Locke and David Hume. Their tradition was continued into the twentieth century by philosophers such as Bertrand Russell, but it is primarily in the contexts of logical positivism and the scientific method that empiricism was then discussed.

Logical positivism consisted of a set of ideas put forward by a group of philosophers known as the "Vienna Circle" in the early part of the twentieth century. Fundamental to logical positivism was the "verifiability principle," which asserts that the meaning of a proposition is identified with the method of verifying it. Before reaching the question of whether a proposition is true or false, we should determine what we mean by it; and then we should be able to indicate the facts which should be obtained if the thesis is true and their difference from other facts which should be obtained if the proposition is not true. According to this theory, to be cognitively meaningful, the facts in a sentence must be either analytically or empirically verifiable. C. I. Lewis agreed, saying that we need intelligibility of a proposition

> not only verbally and logically but in the further sense that one can specify those empirical items which would determine the applicability of the concept or constitute the verification of the proposition. What cannot satisfy this demand is to be regarded as meaningless.[25]

Rudolf Carnap, who accepted a variation of the verifiability theory, looked to a proposition's confirmability:

> A term (predicate) is a legitimate scientific term (has cognitive content, is empirically meaningful) if and only if a sentence applying the term to a given instance can possibly be confirmed to at least some degree.[26]

The scientific method is also fundamentally empirical. Verification by means of the scientific method involves confirming or disconfirming hypotheses through tests which heavily utilize present perception. Scientific conclusions are regarded as valid only if they accurately reflect the tested observations. A critical attitude supplements the inductive techniques of the method, for exacting standards are demanded in order to guard against error and allow for the replication of the tests.

After a slow beginning, the scientific method has flourished and become the principal contemporary means for verifying truths about the natural world. Its early proponents, like the early advocates of most strong ideas, met with little acceptance and harsh opposition. Galileo, for example, believed that observation and experiment were able to establish scientific knowledge,[27] but he was forced to recant and was persecuted for those opinions. Pierre Laplace was also an innovator in the early nineteenth century when he wrote that "induction, analogy, hypothesis founded upon facts and rectified continually by new observations" were "the principal means for arriving at a truth."[28]

We use induction more than some of us might expect (for example, in deciding when it is time to harvest a crop or what to wear to a dance), for induction is a major form of confirmation of truth which we regularly apply in our daily lives. Inductive reasoning is accepted as a means of confirming or disconfirming the truth of assertions because its process has been generally deemed to be reliable.

4. INTUITION

The nature of the mental faculty of intuition is difficult to describe in words, even though we continually witness its occurrence and its results. Some philosophers, in fact, believe that it is futile to try to understand intuition by rational means; for as R. G. H. Siu noted, to pursue intuition rationally is to remain in the realm of the rational.[29] Notwithstanding that admonition, however, I will now try to make several observations about the relationship between intuition and confirmation.

Many philosophers have discussed the nature and merits of intuition. Blaise Pascal argued that we reason based upon intuited first principles and that we can proceed to new truths only when we use intuited truths in that manner.[30] Henri Bergson characterized intuition as contact with inner essence and inner selves, saying that "By intuition is meant the kind of intellectual sympathy by which one places oneself within an object in order to coincide with what is unique in it and consequently inexpressible."[31] Benedetto Croce contrasted intuition, as a nonconceptual form of knowledge, with conceptual or intelligible knowledge,[32] saying that it is "the awareness of a particular image either of outward sense (a person or a thing) or of inner sense (an emotion or a mood)."[33] Henri Poincare wrote that with intuition one has "the ability to see the goal from afar,"[34] and phenomenologists have also characterized it as a "seeing of some extraordinary kind."[35] William Gordon wrote that "Intuition is an inner judgment made by the individual about a concept relative to a problem on which he is working."[36] Siu said that intuitive understanding is grasped as an immediate, total apprehension: it is "an instantaneous integration of unexpressed human thought."[37]

In addition to the philosophers who have expressly accepted intuition both as a source and as a means for the confirmation of truth, many others have recognized that intuition performs such functions during their discussions of other issues. For example, David Hume, in disputing that a rational inference can be found to support the inductive reliance on uniform prior experience as justification for the prediction of uniformity in future experience, said that "The connection between these propositions is not intuitive."[38] Alfred Tarski wrote that our intuitions about when a statement is true can be a guide for us in this process.[39] As more recent examples, Lawrence BonJour contends that intuitions merit some weight in a number of determinations we make,[40] and Frederick Schmitt wrote that "disquotational deflationism runs afoul of strong intuitions and thus must be rejected."[41]

Distinguishing intuitions from other kinds of thoughts is not always easy, but according to Michael Drury, intuitions can be recognized by the unique feelings that accompany them:

> Intuitive comprehension may be felt, but the feeling is based upon long past language and takes instant form in words, which is all that makes it available to us. From my own observations, I would say what one feels at the instant of intuition is awe at the suddenness and completeness of the statement rushing into one's mind, rather than an emotional perception preceding the statement.[42]

William Gordon also thought that personal reactions were the means of its identification, saying that there is an excitement and feeling of pleasure accompanying its selection and signaling a valid intuition.[43]

I have some difficulty with several of these descriptions. For example, if intuition has a "nonconceptual" nature, it is so fleeting as to be inconsequential. We are only aware of specific intuitions as results, when they have either become verbalized as assertions or become actualized as feelings or thoughts which can thereby be readily verbalized. Intuitions occur when we come up with assertive conclusions without having been aware of any of the major inferential (or perhaps biochemical or spiritual) processes which may have been involved. Intuitions may somehow derive from inferential shortcuts made subconsciously by the mind (or the brain), but the bottom line is that we are presented with an intuition essentially either as a finished assertion or as a feeling or impression which may fairly easily be asserted.

Regardless of its ultimate nature, however, we have found that intuition is a source of truth because it is capable of producing assertions which turn out to be true. Intuition is also another means which we may use for the confirmation of truth because of the inferential support we find through deductions like "My intuitions about this kind of thing have often turned out to be true; therefore, because I have intuited 'A is B,' the probability of the truth of 'A is B' is thereby supported." Intuition used as a major premise in this manner is thus able to provide confirming support for its own products.

5. EXTERNAL AUTHORITY

By "external authority" I mean to refer to sources of potentially accurate information about facts and about the truth or falsity of facts coming from someone or something other than ourselves. This type of confirmation is sometimes referred to as "epistemic authority," but I prefer to focus on those who provide such assertions rather than on its content. It is also sometimes referred to as "testimony"; but because a great deal of testimony is indiscriminate and erroneous, the actual source of confirmation which is available to us is narrower than that. For these purposes, we seek input not from everyone who might volunteer an opinion but rather only from those who are in good positions to provide helpful information in a confirmation effort–that is, from those who are "authorities" on the issue in question. When we want help from external authorities, we refer to others who we have reason to believe may have authoritative knowledge about a particular fact.

External authority functions as confirmation when we correctly accept an assertion as being true or as being more probably true than not because of the support which has been given to it by someone else. The general inference here is made along the following lines: "Others who are particularly knowledgeable about the facts underlying an assertion can be good sources of information which can help us determine whether that assertion is true; KP is an authority on statements like 'X is Y'; KP says that statement 'X is Y' is true; therefore, 'X is Y' is probably true." An example of the application of this type of inference is "Dictionaries are reliable sources for correct definitions of words; because the dictionary says so, it is true that a definition of 'authority' is 'reliability of a source or witness.'"

In the past, royal and religious authorities were widely accepted as being the ultimate sources for the confirmation of truth. As civilization has evolved, however, so have our sources of external authority. Many people now tend to consider church and state as less conclusive validators of truth; but, at the same time, we have expanded the number and types of external authorities upon whom we are willing to rely. For example, we now frequently accept the assertions of specialists, such as professors, surgeons, researchers, and patent lawyers, about things in their respective fields of expertise.

External authority is a widely used and highly useful form of truth confirmation. Because we accept the major premise-that what carefully selected external authorities tell us about the truth or falsity of assertions is often reliable-we are able to confirm specific truths for ourselves through middle steps (like "The truth of assertion 'A is B' is broadly supported by reliable external authorities") and help us arrive at appropriate conclusions about the truth or falsity of those statements (e.g., "Therefore, assertion 'A is B' is true").

6. FAITH

Faith and its functions have been continuously discussed over the millennia by virtually everyone, including many theologians and philosophers. One group has argued that faith is dependent upon revelation-that, as Augustinianism held, faith enters our minds through divine illumination, which would make faith purely a matter of external authority. An alternative explanation, at least for products of faith which may not be revealed truths, was provided by Teilhard de Chardin, who described it as an intellectual synthesis:

> In my view, the essential note of the psychological act of faith is to perceive as possible, and accept as more probable, a conclusion which, in spatial width or temporal extension, cannot be contained in any analytical premises. . . . To believe, is to develop an act of synthesis whose first origin is inapprehensible.[44]

Faith, for the purpose of the confirmation of truth, is thus the firm belief in the accuracy of a given assertion for otherwise unspecific and undefinable reasons. It is distinguished from other forms of belief by the strength and endurance of the assurance that the believer feels in its truth. Assertions accepted on faith are not completely obvious, nor are they clear and distinct, nor are they logically necessary. Indeed, such assertions have not, by definition, been fully substantiated by any of the other forms of confirmation, or else we would say that they were confirmed in those other ways. But because of faith, we find ourselves willing to accept certain assertions as being true despite the insufficiency of those other proofs. Since this general premise (in the form of "We may find valid support for some truths through faith") allows inferences about the truth of propositions supported by faith (e.g., "I have faith that assertion 'X is Y' is true; therefore, 'X is Y' is true," faith constitutes a separate form of confirmation.

Many philosophers and theologians, including Soren Kierkegaard and Thomas Aquinas, have suggested that religious truths, with their sources in faith and revelation, are a separate species of truth. Faith is most commonly associated with religion, but epistemologically it encompasses a much wider range of subjects. In addition to various religious tenets, we accept many other assertions at least in part on faith because of their otherwise insufficient confirmations. For example, the fundamental assumption of induction-that nature has an underlying uniformity-has significant, but not total, empirical support. Therefore, when we accept and employ the principle of the uniformity of nature, we are doing so in part on faith. Because we have not seen and cannot see or comprehend all of nature, we must use faith to extend what we do know of nature to all space and time. In spite of the forcefulness with which we usually recognize present sensory perceptions, faith plays a role even in our acceptance of the reality of the external world; for the last step in concluding that external objects exist from the premise of our internal perceptions of sense data is not a necessary one. We cannot completely prove, for example, that an evil demon has not created our sensations without a corresponding world, and we cannot completely prove that we are not brains in vats that are being stimulated into thinking that such a world exists.[45] Thus, that step is taken (and we all take it) in part on faith. William James commented on another manner in which reason is dependent upon faith in this way:

> Science herself consults her heart when she lays it down that the infinite ascertainment of fact and correction of false belief are the supreme goods of man. Challenged, science can only repeat it oracularly or else prove it by showing that such ascertainment and correction bring man all sorts of other goods which man's heart in turn declares.[46]

We should conclude that faith is a form of confirmation not only because many assertions upon which we heavily depend fall far short of being totally validated by other means of confirmation but also because some of the other forms of confirmation upon which we rely are based upon grounds which are themselves at least partially dependent upon faith (as will be discussed further in Chapter 3).

7. INTENTION

Intention, a seventh form of confirmation, is extremely limited in the scope of its useful application. Nevertheless, while a skeptical reaction can be expected to the suggestion that what we intend (or desire or hope for) could be the validation of anything ("You can hope for the moon, but that won't make it true"), because there is some validity in specific circumstances for the inference, "I intend for 'A is B' to occur; therefore, 'A is B' is now and will also later be true," I believe that it is appropriate to include it.

Often we are not neutral about particular assertions which we make about things we want to have or events which we hope will occur, and we will want our statements about those things to be confirmed or disconfirmed, depending upon our personal preferences. That we employ intention to some extent as a means of confirming the truth of an assertion becomes more apparent when we say things like, "It *is* going to happen, I'll make sure of it!"

Nevertheless, because of its limited scope, if anyone were to object to the inclusion of intention as one of the potentially useful forms of truth confirmation, its deletion would do no significant damage to the validity or use of the rest of the framework that has been set out in this chapter. Indeed, a six-form framework should be able to do virtually all the heavy lifting in confirmations or disconfirmations of most assertions which may be true or false.

The different ways in which we inferentially confirm or disconfirm the truth of assertions which have been discussed here are all valid tools which may be used in our efforts to do so. When each of them should be used with different types of assertions is a critical issue which will be further addressed in Part II; but next I want to expand on the reasons why each of these is effective as a means of truth confirmation.

NOTES

1. I will use "assertion," "statement," and "proposition" indiscriminately because they all carry the meaning of a formulation in language that affirms or denies something about some subject matter. I do not believe that the debates about their differences are germane for my purposes, and the use of a new generic term that might cover all of them seems contrived (e.g., "truthbearers").

2. R. G. H. Siu, *The Tao of Science: An Essay of Western Knowledge and Eastern Wisdom* (New York: The Technology Press, 1957).

3. Pitirim A. Sorokin, *Social Philosophies in an Age of Crisis* (Boston: Beacon Press, 1950), p. 307.

4. C. I. Lewis, "Experience and Meaning," *Readings in Philosophical Analysis*, Herbert Feigl and Wilfrid Sellars, eds. (New York: Appleton-Century-Crofts, 1949), pp. 137–138.

5. The field of psychology has, of course, provided numerous studies of the same phenomena from different perspectives.

6. A. N. Prior, "History of Logic," *The Encyclopedia of Philosophy*, vol. 4, p. 517.

7. Will Durant, *The Mansions of Philosophy* (Garden City, NY: Garden City Pub. House, 1941), pp. 26–27. See also Harry Allen Overstreet, "The Basal Principle of Truth-Evaluation," University of California Pubs., Philosophy, vol. 1, No. 12, p. 245.

8. See, e.g., Albert E. Blumberg, "Modern Logic," *The Encyclopedia of Philosophy*, vol.5, pp. 12–34.

9. R. A. Markus, "St. Augustine," *The Encyclopedia of Philosophy*, vol. 1, p. 201.

10. Descartes, *A Discourse on Method*, p. 21.

11. Gottfried Leibniz, *Philosophical Papers and Letters*, 2nd ed., Leroy E. Leomker, trans. (Dordrecht, Holland: D. Reidel Publishing Co., 1969), p. 43.

12. Mark, *Spinoza's Theory of Truth*, p. 37.

13. Dagobert D. Runes, ed., *The Dictionary of Philosophy* (New York: Philosophical Library, 1942), p. 322.

14. William James, *The Meaning of Truth* (New York: Greenwood Press, 1968), p. 89.

15. Ibid., p. 82.

16. Ralph C. S. Walker, *The Coherence Theory of Truth* (London: Routledge, 1989).

17. Y. P. Mei, "Mo Tzu," *The Encyclopedia of Philosophy*, vol. 5, p. 410.

18. Brand Blanshard, "The Coherence Theory of Truth," *Readings in Contemporary Philosophy*, James L. Jarrett, Jr., et al., eds. (New York: Henry Holt & Co., 1954), p. 34. See also Nicholas Rescher, *The Coherence Theory of Truth* (Oxford: Clarendon Press, 1973).

19. Arthur Kenyon Rogers, *What Is Truth?* (Yale University Press, 1923), p. 26.

20. Martin Johnson, *Science and the Meaning of Truth* (London: Faber & Faber, 1946), p. 15.

21. Pierre Teilhard de Chardin, *How I Believe*, Rene Hague, trans. (New York: Harper & Row, 1969), p. 83, n. 7.

22. W. V. Quine, "Two Dogmas of Empiricism," *Philosophical Review* 60 (1951), p. 38.

23. C. S. Peirce, "Deduction, Induction, and Hypothesis," *Inductive Logic*, Charles G. Werner, ed. (Dubuque, IA: Kendall/Hunt Publishing Co., 1973), p. 111.

24. George K. Strodach, *Epicurus, The Extant Remains* (Evanston, IL: Northwestern University Press, 1963), pp. 30, 38.

25. Lewis, "Experience and Meaning," p. 128.

26. Rudolf Carnap, "Truth and Confirmation," *Readings in Philosophical Analysis*, p. 123.

27. Ernan McMullin, ed., *Galileo: Man of Science* (New York: Basic Books, Inc., 1969), pp. 306–310.

28. R. Harre, "Pierre Simon de Laplace," *The Encyclopedia of Philosophy*, vol. 4, p. 393.

29. Siu, *The Tao of Science*, pp. 74–75.

30. Ernest Mortimer, *Blaise Pascal* (London: Methuen & Co. Ltd.,1959), p. 209.

31. Henri Bergson, *An Introduction to Metaphysics*, as quoted in *Basic Problems of Philosophy*, Daniel J. Bronstein, et al., eds. (New York: Prentice Hall, 1956), p. 34.

32. Benedetto Croce, *Breviary of Aesthetics: Four Lectures*, Hiroko Fudemoto, trans. (University of Toronto Press, 2007), p. 15.

33. H. S. Harris, "Benedetto Croce," *The Encyclopedia of Philosophy*, vol. 2, p. 264.

34. Michael Drury, *The Inward Sea* (New York: Doubleday, 1972), p. 19.

35. See, e.g., *Readings in Contemporary Philosophy*, p. 442.

36. William J. J. Gordon, *Synectics* (New York: Harper and Row, 1961), p. 156.

37. Siu, *The Tao of Science*, p. 75.

38. David Hume, *An Inquiry Concerning Human Understanding*, Tom L. Beauchamp, ed. (Oxford: Clarendon Press, 2000), p. 30.

39. Wilfrid Hodges, "Tarski's Truth Definitions," *The Stanford Encyclopedia of Philosophy* (Summer 2006 Edition), Edward L. Zalta, ed., URL = <http://plato.stanford.edu/archives/sum2006/entries/tarski/truth/>.

40. Lawrence BonJour, *In Defense of Pure Reason* (Cambridge University Press, 1998), p. 104.

41. Frederick Schmitt, *Truth: A Primer* (Boulder, CO: Westview Press, 1995), p. 132.

42. Drury, *The Inward Sea*, pp. 82–83.

43. Gordon, *Synectics*, p. 156.

44. Teilhard de Chardin, *How I Believe*, pp. 13–15.

45. The evil-demon argument is that we cannot be sure that we are not being misled in all of our mental activities by an evil demon which is merely making it appear, for example, that the sun is shining through the window. Brain-in-a-vat debates are a modernized manner of rearguing Bishop Berkeley's contention that we cannot really know what, if anything, exists beyond our minds and its mental conceptions of things. If a mad scientist were to place a brain in a vat and stimulate it electrochemically, then, arguably, that brain could be having every perception which I believe that I am having of the external world.

46. William James, "The Will to Believe," *Gateway to the Great Books*, Robert M. Hutchens, et al., eds. (Chicago: Encyclopedia Brittanica, 1952), pp. 51–52.

Chapter Three

Confirming the Means

Each of the seven types of confirmation which may be used as a means of verifying the truth of assertions needs to be closely examined for effectiveness and reliability. We should test all of the inferential tools which we propose to employ for the discovery and confirmation of truth in order to determine whether-and to what extent-they really can do so. To do this, we need to search for all of the support or opposition which may exist for the use of each of them as a major premise in our confirmation efforts.

The tests for each of these means must necessarily utilize the same seven kinds of inferences which were set out above for the confirmation of truth generally; for if those methods work in our searches for other kinds of factual truth, they should also work when we look specifically at propositions about the methods which can help us distinguish between true and false statements. It is also the case that these are the only effective means which are available to us for the confirmation of any truth.

1. PRESENT PERCEPTION

The first of these types of truth-confirming inferences begins with "It is true that an effective means for confirming truth is present perception." One reason why we have come to believe that present perception of personal internal and external conditions or events can provide an effective major premise and be used as a basis for the valid confirmation of truth is experiential and thus inductive: we accept the recognition of present perception as a confirmation of the truth of statements about those perceptions because that is the primary way in which we have learned to evaluate them for accuracy. We have discerned that our senses have generally been accurate-as far as we know and as far as we can know-in telling us things about the external world, and we are therefore willing to accept our recognition of a new sensation as a type of confirmation which is useful when we are trying to ascertain the truth of an assertion about any such phenomena. The same thing holds true for our present mental states: through our experience, we have come to identify different kinds of feelings, and when we become aware that those feelings are recurring, we know them and the accuracy of statements about them by recognizing them. Present perception is therefore validated first and foremost by our personal experience: we cannot well or long ignore, for example, trees that stand in our way. When we perceive solid obstacles in front of us, we will believe that if we do not deviate from our current path in some way, we will run into them, with negative results. Justification of the validity of present sense perception is thus provided by our lifetimes of experience. Similarly, the recognition process has worked well for assertions about perceptions of our internal mental states. If I recognize that I am feeling tired, then I am justified in concluding that it is true that I am feeling tired because of the reliability of similar recognitions of such perceptions which I have had in the past.

That we originally confirm present perceptions by recognizing them is further illustrated by how we *reconfirm* them: by casting a second glance, by listening closely, by asking ourselves how we *really* feel, and so forth. Indeed, if we recognize the same thing repeatedly, testing it over and over as we are able to do so at different points in time, we feel even more assured that the assertions about our recognition of each of those present perceptions have been accurately made.

The acceptability of this method for confirming the truth or falsity of assertions about our present perceptions is also illustrated by the manners in which we *disconfirm* statements about our present internal states or about sensations involving the external world. The primary manner in which we disconfirm a statement about such a perception is by looking for it and finding that it is not really there. We all know that we have sometimes been fooled about some of our physical sensations-and we all should be willing to agree that we sometimes could again be fooled in the future-by such things as dreams, illusions, hallucinations, or mistaken interpretations (because of, for example, confusion or fatigue). We also sometimes err-and we could err again in the future-with regard to our present mental states due to the kinds of same things. But most sensory and perceptual errors and aberrations are discoverable in the short term if we remain consciously aware of and alert for the specific types of things which we know might cause us to be mistaken and then carefully look for them, particularly when we suspect that they might be present. We can usually tell when we are fatigued, for example; and if we determine that we are, then we can consider the impact of our fatigue as we reconsider an initial perception about a present mental state. In any event, if we take a closer look at anything which we think may be an accurate present perception and we are unable to recognize it again–and particularly if we see something that helps us understand why that initial perception may have been in error–we may disconfirm the initial assertion which we made about that perception.

The recognition of present perception as a method for confirming the truth of certain types of assertions is also supported by memory-specifically, by memories of perceptions which we had in the past which are (or were) confirmed by our subsequent experience. We not only know of the validity of present perception generally because we can test it in the present, but we can also add to that body of support the many recollections which we have of reconfirmations of the accuracy of such perceptions through subsequent or repeated perceptions of them.

Another major support for the validity of our recognition of present perception as a means of finding and confirming truth is provided by external authority. We are taught from the cradle by others how to identify our sensations and feelings; but perhaps more importantly, we are also taught and shown that our perceptions are generally reliable and that we should trust them. At the same time, we learn how to recognize and deal with some of the limitations which exist for this means of truth confirmation from those who are sharing with us their experience and knowledge about how we can better find and confirm such truths, particularly in difficult situations. We are also frequently provided with confirming or disconfirming input from others on specific assertions about our present perceptions when they have access to the same objects (e.g., "Those socks aren't black, they're dark blue"). Other people who are credible thus provide us with additional reasons to accept present perception as a valid means for us to use when we are trying to confirm the truth or falsity of these types of assertions.

Faith is involved here as well because of the limitations on the support provided for this proposition by other sources. Faith performs a role in getting us beyond "evil demon" and "brain-in-a-vat" arguments and contentions that we cannot know "things-in-themselves," to the extent that these present issues when considering the validity of perception in the confirmation of truth.

We also use deduction in this analysis not only in a procedural manner in combination with present perceptions as we interpret them (to arrive at, for example, "That object is a carrot"), but also in concluding from the above analysis that present perception is a valid means of confirming truth.

I have not identified any substantive input from intuition on the issue of perception as validation, for I did not intuit the major premise that is provided by present perception. Intention is not of any assistance here, either; my intentions about this form of confirmation are irrelevant to it. Nevertheless, because of the corroboration of the capacity of present perception to confirm truth that can be obtained primarily through induction, memory, and external authority, but also to some extent through faith, this method should be deemed to have passed the test of its potential for validity when it is applied to statements which are made about our currently perceived internal and external worlds.

2. MEMORY

As with present perception, we accept memory as a means of confirmation in part because our minds have always worked that way and because they have to work that way. Without memory, we could not think or function as we do. Memory is an inherent *sine qua non* of our minds' activities. We could not otherwise recognize similarities or differences (except when all the objects or ideas being compared are completely available in the present). We could not name anything so that we could later refer to it by its symbol, and thus language would be impossible. We could not retain anything even about the immediate past, and we thus could never learn anything at all without it. All meaning, coherence, consistency, and differentiation would be lost, so that our remaining capacities would place us on the mental level of the lower forms of animal life. Consequently, the existence of language and the existence of meaning themselves help confirm memory as a valid method for testing the truth for assertions about the past.

Bertrand Russell, in *The Analysis of Mind*, wrote that feelings of pastness and the sense we have of the relative passages of time are also supportive of the validity of memory as a means of knowing truths about the past.[1] These things recognize memory at work by how it works. Russell also argued that our feelings of familiarity with certain memories can, when sufficiently strong, support our conclusions about their accuracy. More recently, John Pollock and Joseph Cruz wrote that when someone seems to remember something, that is in itself a separate reason for believing that the "something" indeed occurred in the past.[2]

The validity of memory as a method of finding and confirming truths about the past can also be regularly and repeatedly supported by presently testing it, which then provides inductive substantiation for it. For example, "I remember leaving my pencil on the table, and . . . aha! There it is!" Cumulatively, such individual tests of remembrances which we are able to later confirm provide justification for the validity of memory as a means of determining the truth or falsity of present assertions about the past. Its utility, as supported by subsequent verifications of tentatively remembered assertions, is also accepted on a pragmatic basis: a correctly recollected memory provides successful confirmation of the remembered fact. This experiential justification is normally left unstated; but because we have learned that our memories have most often been accurate, we usually accept a specific remembrance as sufficient confirmation of a personal recollection in and of itself.

Finally, external authorities provide significant support for the validity of memory as the basis for the general premise which we use in this approach to the confirmation of truth. We test our memories all of our lives not only by ourselves but also through the assistance of other people (frequently beginning with the words, "Do you remember . . . ?"). Because others often remember the same things and because they are able to provide even further support for the accuracy of a given memory (e.g., through a writing made contemporaneously with the event or a photograph they have taken of it), we are further justified in believing that the remembrance of something is a useful test of the truth of statements about things which have occurred in the past.

Memories do, of course, fade and fail. Therefore, we frequently need to seek additional support for or refutation of assertions about particular personal memories through other forms of confirmation. We often use external authority and rational verification for that purpose. However, while we cannot have complete confidence that every memory we have is valid, we do justifiably find the inference, "If I remember A, then A occurred," to be supportive of the truth of assertions about the past.

3. REASON

a. Deduction

The validity of the deductive inference is supported by four major lines of argument. The first is that its justification is a matter of self-evidence. Ludwig Wittgenstein said that "It is the characteristic mark of logical propositions that one can perceive in the symbol alone that they are true."[3] Given my attitude toward self-evidence arguments, however, I find it fortunate that the three other reasons are more inferential than that.

The second type of support is provided through an appeal to social accord-to external authorities, in other words. As W. V. Quine put it:

> Logical truths, being tied to the grammar and not to the lexicon, will be among the truths on which all speakers are likeliest to agree. . . . The logical truths, or the simple ones, will go without saying; everyone will unhesitatingly assent to them if asked.[4]

Another reason we accept deduction is because we have experienced a great deal of success with it in the past, and, on that basis, we expect it to continue to work in the future. This constitutes a confirmation of deduction through inductive logic.

Finally, acceptance of deduction is urged on the basis of the logical principles of non-contradiction and intelligibility, for we cannot "think" without them. William Werkmeister said that the proof of deductive logic may be accomplished by "showing that the laws in question cannot be consistently denied so long as we accept as valid any logical implications of this denial."[5] Along the same lines, Josiah Royce asserted that deductive logic cannot be rationally rejected because the truths of pure logic are those "such that to deny them is to assert them under a new form."[6]

Deductive logic is thus validated as a means of confirmation of the truth or falsity of assertions by inductive, experiential proof, by external authority, and by several key deductive arguments themselves. These major supports provide adequate justification for our acceptance of deductive logic as a valid means to be used in the confirmation of truth.

b. Induction

We support our acceptance of induction as a valid method of verifying truth in several different ways, as well. A good deal of that support is pragmatic: we must use induction in order to live. Hans Reichenbach wrote:

> We try induction because we want to act-and he who wants to act cannot wait until the future has become observational knowledge. . . . Induction is the best instrument of action known to us.[7]

Induction is useful to us in this sense because it provides many of the premises for our deductions. Francis Parker and Henry Veatch suggested that "Ultimately it is through induction and only through induction that true premises may be supplied for deduction."[8] P. W. Bridgman wrote:

> As usually practiced, the premises of our deductions are obtained by inductive methods. When we say that all men are mortal we very seldom have behind us a verification by observation of all men, but the statement usually implies an inductive generalization of some sort.[9]

A second type of justification entails an inductive proof of itself: because induction has proven to be reliable in the past in verifying assertions, we believe that we are justified in concluding that induction will continue to be a valid method of confirmation in the future. As stated by Bridgman, "There is no ultimate justification for the procedure except that in the past it has worked."[10]

We are able to find verification of this form of confirmation through external authority, as well. The statement of W. V. Quine quoted above with reference to deductive logic (that logical truths are those on which everyone is likeliest to agree) applies to inductive as well as deductive reasoning.

We thus mainly rely on these pragmatic, inductive, and external-authority justifications when we accept the role of induction in the confirmation of truth.

c. The Limits of Rational Verification

Rational verification–through both deduction and induction-is not, as some would have it, the be-all and end-all of the confirmation of truth, because it is limited by its unproven assumptions, by the extra-rational influences upon its use, by its circumscribed scope, and by gaps in its ultimate confirmability. Because rational verification is given such wide deference, it is appropriate at this point to review these limitations in order to keep its capacities in perspective.

All reasoning depends upon certain presuppositions. Deduction presumes, for instance, the validity of its premises and the values of consistency and non-contradiction, while the fundamental assumption of induction is the uniformity of nature. In addition, both forms of reason assume such things as causation, which is a significant factor in inference and which is, to some extent, rationally unprovable.[11] C. S. Peirce commented on reason's foundational assumptions as follows:

> Find a scientific man who proposes to get along without metaphysics . . . and you have found one whose doctrines are thoroughly vitiated by the crude and uncriticized metaphysics with which they are packed.[12]

Because logic must be articulated in order to be understood, reason must also work through language. Language is the system through which we organize, formulate, express, and communicate our thoughts and feelings. It is an inexact system, however, containing potential errors of misidentifications and other misunderstandings. As Jose Ortega y Gasset put it:

> No statement is an adequate summation of its intention, but merely an abbreviation, an insinuation of what it means to say. All articulated language partially states or considers as stated many things that act upon the thinker, that form part of his thought but are either "left unsaid because they are assumed," or that he himself, because they seem so self-evident to him, neglects to pursue.[13]

Language also brings other problems. Wilhelm Dilthey noted that "To understand a word we must understand the language, yet to understand a language we must have come to understand the words that constitute it."[14] Even ostensive definitions are neither simple nor independently valid. As Wittgenstein observed, they "presuppose a prior grasp of language," including a preexisting linguistic framework (e.g., the role of words in language and the function of certain sounds as words) and an understanding of the other terms in the definition.[15] Furthermore, different languages reflect different social influences. Wilhelm von Humboldt said that languages contain deep-rooted subjective views of the world and imply spiritual attitudes which control the formation of concepts.[16] Henri Poincare wrote that we could not free ourselves from the language we have learned even if we were to try:

> Everyone carries in his mind his own conception of the world, of which he cannot so easily rid himself. We must, for instance, use language; and our language is made up only of preconceived ideas and cannot be otherwise. Only these are unconscious preconceived ideas, a thousand times more dangerous than the others.[17]

Some psychologists[18] and sociologists[19] have argued that our epistemological orientations vary among different societies and that no society can operate in a manner which does not favor certain approaches or methodologies over others.

Another limitation on reason is that it is dependent upon other forms of confirmation, and indeed, it cannot function without them. The most essential non-rational forms of confirmation for reason are faith (for example, in supporting its underlying presuppositions discussed above, such as the uniformity of nature), present perception (in presenting data for rational consideration), and external authority (in providing information, context, and perspective).

Reason also has limited extension: it is inadequate when it is asked to verify truths involving many of life's major issues. Kant called some of the contradictions with which we are confronted-each of which possesses rationally defensible positions-"antimonies" (like "The world had a beginning in time," and "The world did not have a beginning in time").[20] Similarly, a tenet of Hindu philosophy is that "Life cannot be fully comprehended by logical reason."[21] Through reason, we have been unable to understand infinity and eternity, and we have been unable to prove God's existence or nonexistence or life or nonlife after death. Nicolas of Cusa argued that we are simply unable to reach absolute truth: "Our intellect . . . never grasps the truth with such precision that it could not be apprehended with infinitely greater precision."[22] Surely there must be answers to the ultimate questions posed above; but just as surely, a number of them have-at least as yet-proven to be inaccessible to rational determination.

In the strictest sense, therefore, reason is simply not completely confirmable. Besides relying on unproven assumptions and accepting some of its primary directions in part through acts of faith, no logical system can be proven to be conclusively valid. Godel's Theorem affirms this principle as follows:

> It is impossible to prove that a logical system at least as complicated as arithmetic contains no concealed contradictions by using only theorems which are derivable within the system. . . . It is necessary to use theorems which can be proved only by going outside the system . . . and then to prove these new principles do not conceal contradiction one must use new principles beyond them. The regress has no end-one has languages and meta-languages without limit.[23]

In addition to these general criticisms of reason, both deduction and induction have been separately subjected to extensive criticisms. The specific limitations of deductive logic have been stated in a number of ways. One criticism from a negative perspective is the fact that deductive conclusions, which necessarily follow from their premises, are "presupposed" by their premises. Carrying it one step further, Sextus Empiricus characterized these arguments as circular reasoning, because the truth of each conclusion must already be decided once the criterion of the major premise has been ascertained.[24] A second criticism is that deduction cannot establish its own premises: while a premise may have been deductively proven through a prior inference, ultimately, it may not be deductively produced. We must seek confirmation of each deduction's premises elsewhere-for example, in induction or from external authorities. Having done so, however, we must then agree with Pyrrho that all of deduction's certainty is relative to something that deduction itself cannot find out.[25] A third limitation of deduction is that formal deductive logic suffers from triviality in that it has limited application to reality because much of life is too ambiguous for it. When we try to find the major philosophical problems which have been resolved-or even addressed-by formal logic, we usually find that formal logic has primarily considered only itself.

Several of the specific rational tests for truth have been subjected to regular criticisms, as well. The "clarity and distinctness" criterion has problems which limit its effectiveness as such a test. This criterion assumes that the prototype proposition is true, but that may not necessarily be so; and all of the results of such a test would be invalidated if the prototype turned out to be false. It is also a subjective test, depending upon personal-and therefore varying-evaluations of "obviousness" and "clarity." Finally, even its proponents have not always relied on this test. Arthur Kenyon Rogers accused such philosophers of "surreptitiously" bringing in common sense to justify their conclusions.[26] Because of these problems, along with those pointed out in Chapter 1, the clear and distinct test is not a completely satisfactory criterion of truth. Nevertheless, as a practical matter, when an assertion appears to be "obvious," we do routinely use that inference ("If Assertion 'A is B' appears obvious or appears clearly and distinctly to be true, then 'A is B' is true") as a means of confirming its truth; and we often later find that we were justified in so using it. It remains, therefore, one of the effective rational tools which we can use for the confirmation of the truth of an assertion.

The pragmatic approach to truth also has substantial limitations, beginning with its inherent subjectivity; for what is "satisfying" or "useful" to one person need not be so to another. In fact, we are more likely to disagree on what may be satisfactory or useful than on what may be true, because "satisfaction" and "usefulness" are more directly attuned to individual desires and emotions. We can all think of assertions about many things which are or were satisfying to us (e.g., the good meal I had last night), but our satisfaction with them does not seem to have any bearing upon their truth whatsoever (other than a truth about the satisfaction that is involved). Brand Blanshard wrote that with pragmatism, "meaning would be confined to each individual stream of experience."[27] Bertrand Russell, who noted that what "working" is supposed to mean is ambiguous,[28] observed that "useful" is simply not equivalent to the common meaning of the word "true."[29] Furthermore, even a false idea may still "succeed" in some way. For example, if I see what looks like smoke coming from an object and exclaim "It's hot, don't touch it!" but it turns out that the "smoke" was due to an extremely cold temperature, the first part of the assertion was false, but the assertion as a whole was nevertheless both useful and satisfying if it kept you from touching it. Nevertheless, we sometimes use a pragmatic inference to confirm an assertion, especially in practical matters (like the truth we seek when we change a sparkplug: if the new sparkplug works, we conclude that our assertions about how to change it were true). Consequently, just because pragmatism does not succeed as an independent theory of truth on its own does not mean that it has not provided a useful tool for the confirmation of truth.

The coherence theory and its approach to truth have been criticized on several major grounds, as well. One objection is that it must always assume-but that it is almost always not able to prove-the truth of the accepted assertions to which any "new" assertion is being compared. Consequently, the set of statements to which the new one may cohere would not be grounded in some sure way in truth themselves. How those may be distinguished as the appropriate test for the new assertion, as opposed to another set of different cohering statements, is not clear, especially when the new assertion might cohere with both of them. As a result, its critics argue that the coherence theory favors consistency above truth, because the "body" of accepted truths may prove to be false. As George Santayana put it:

> To reduce truth to coherence is to deny truth, and to usurp that name for a certain comfort and self-complacency in mere thinking. Why trouble about truth, if I can be sure of never discovering my error?[30]

In recognition of this problem and in an attempt to avoid its complete demise, J. L. Mackie referred to coherence as a "temporary criterion," arguing that it yields only an as-yet-unchallenged claim to the title of truth.[31]

Two other major criticisms of the coherence theory are that it is merely circular reasoning and that it suffers from infinite regress. To respond to these criticisms, we first need to consider how we think of human knowledge. We often misconceptualize knowledge (which is our reservoir of justified true belief) by thinking of it only in linear terms. We tend to measure how much we know in progressions which we can connect vertically or horizontally. For example, we think we learn math by beginning with addition and subtraction, then by moving on to multiplication and division, and so on. Many of our specific inquiries appear to proceed from point A to point B and then to point C; and our lives develop linearly over time in calendar progressions. But knowledge is not well analogized to single lines or chains because it extends in many directions and involves complex interconnections. The interrelationships which develop among our separate bits of knowledge create innumerable ties among all of the truths that we know. Furthermore, linear conceptions of knowledge must ultimately rely on "first truths"; but no one assertion can be the sole genesis or "first truth" of all human knowledge, for every assertion is based upon pre-existing and assumed knowledge and mental faculties.[32] That is why I believe that a better spatial analogy for knowledge is a sphere rather than a line: for all specific knowledge is ultimately tied back into itself, and, as our knowledge grows, it is expanding in all directions. This analogy also serves us well when we recognize that our collective knowledge is finite but unbounded, as is a sphere. It is finite because there are and have been a finite number of human beings who have had a finite amount of knowledge up to the present time; but it is unbounded because it is without beginning or ending points and because it is continually capable of further growth, which leads to an expansion of our collective sphere of knowledge. We can always add more to our knowledge of the universe and all that is within it.

If the spherical analogy is accepted, then we can quickly perceive its impact upon the related criticisms of infinite regress and circular reasoning. Infinite regress is a charge that is leveled when the justification of an assertion is not firmly grounded by its initial bases: what appear to be its foundations turn out simply to be assumptions which need to be grounded on other bases, and so on. But if knowledge is an unbounded whole, infinite regress is merely a negative way of describing the normal search for knowledge. As we move from one assertion either forward into its ramifications or backward into its foundations, we are continually learning more about the complex inter-relationships of all knowledge. Therefore, the criticism of infinite regress does not cause me to believe either that such an assertion is false or that the coherence criterion for truth is thereby invalidated, because it is in the nature of knowledge (of time, temples, truth, and all other phenomena) to be tied to other knowledge in forward, backward, and sideways directions.

As for circular reasoning, we should first admit that it is valid reasoning. It is usually rejected or criticized, however, because we do not learn anything new from it (i.e., it is boring knowledge). I must concede that limited circular reasoning (A is B and B is A) provides us with no new knowledge; but it is also true. One way to deal with the real problem of circular reasoning is by expanding the "circle" of assertions under consideration (A is B is C is D . . . is X is Y is Z is A. . . .). But the fact that all knowledge may eventually lead back to itself does not invalidate or disconfirm that knowledge, nor does it undermine the coherence method for the verification of truth. Thus, in spite of its problems, we frequently do and should employ a coherence inference in our attempts to confirm the truth of different assertions. If the assertion "fits in" or "makes sense" in the context of our knowledge of a given field, then we accept that fact as being supportive of that assertion's truth.

While deductive logic may not always be substantively applicable, and while it cannot solve all of the problems which we face in trying to determine the truth of assertions, it is useful to us procedurally every time we deal with a statement which may be true or false. Even though major and minor premises do in a certain sense "presuppose" deductive conclusions, that only means that we should identify and verbalize the things we have accepted and the processes which we have used in arriving at those particular positions. The recognition of the relativity of a conclusion to its premises does not negate or undermine the assistance which we are given in finding particular truths through deductive inferences which allow us to use and apply those premises. Finally, only formal deductive systems (and not deduction itself) are arguably devoted primarily to esoteric matters; for it is also true that no effective reasoning would be possible without deductive logic.

Just as deductive systems cannot conclusively be proven to be valid, neither can inductive systems. Their pragmatic and inductive bases are hardly beyond reproach; and in addition, all induction rests upon an initial, unprovable assumption of the uniformity of nature. Hans Reichenbach wrote that there is no guarantee that induction can achieve its aim because the world may be "so disorderly" that it would be impossible for us to effectively use it[33]: "We must admit . . . that we do not know whether the world is predictable."[34] While acceptance of the uniformity of nature is quite reasonable, it is also-to some extent-an act of faith.

Particular inductive conclusions may always be in error, as well-especially those which are aimed toward the future, when everything may yet turn out unexpectedly. To minimize the possibilities of error, we take certain precautions, like making sure that inductive results have been based upon a sufficient sampling of the members of the classes involved, thereby avoiding the common mistake of making a conclusion before it is warranted. But minimizing the possibility of error is not the same thing as eliminating it.

All of the empirically oriented systems have received significant specific criticisms, as well. Logical positivism, like pragmatism, declined as a movement long ago. Among the causes of its slide were its major limitations, such as its circumscribed applicability. On this point, Josiah Royce noted that, while there are a lot of things that we cannot personally verify, we must still accept many of them as being true.[35] G. A. Rauche argued its triviality, saying that logical positivists, like logicians, had abandoned the search for truth and were content merely to analyze or debate the "truth-functions" of propositions.[36] Still other critics dismissed it just as being coherence in another guise. Karl Popper pointed out that logical positivists could never achieve their goal in making confirmations, for they were too optimistic about finding justifications through positive evidence. (He proposed disconfirmability as an alternative.[37]) Nevertheless, some of the main themes of logical positivism have remained central in the discussion of the confirmation of truth, especially including the necessary tie between confirmability and any declaration of truth.

The scientific method has been more specifically criticized as well. Its restricted scope is recognized in that it is primarily limited to statements about parts of the world which may be objectively tested. Even then science does not resolve some of our greatest mysteries, for sometimes it appears to lead us into unresolvable problems from which there seems to be no scientific escape (e.g., what existed before the Big Bang, what exists outside of our universe, etc.). Furthermore, people sometimes seem to forget that the scientific method is based upon a number of unproven metaphysical presuppositions, such as causation and the uniformity of nature. Another critical observation is that the means of formulating hypotheses is often intuitive, a factor which cuts against any "purely" rational characterization of the scientific method.

40   *Chapter Three*

The fact of error also runs throughout scientific verification. Solomon Diamond wrote:

> Even with the finest instrumentation and the most careful procedures, there is no experiment without error, and hence no science possible which does not recognize error as an inevitable part of its data. When we say "error is inevitable," this is just another way of saying, "the world is complicated."[38]

In addition, it is sometimes asserted that the scientific method is not followed as often as it is alleged to be, or that, in other words, we appropriately use it less frequently than we believe we do. Finally, some say that there are too many methodological variations in the scientific method for a single description of it to suffice. Nevertheless, despite all these limitations, the scientific method is the current champion of empiricism, and it provides the primary substantiation for many of the most significant truths which we accept today.

Reason supplies a number of inferences which we directly use in trying to confirm the truth or falsity of an assertion. From the primary inferences which rely on the strength of these logical tools themselves ("If assertion 'X is Y' is the result of a properly applied deduction or induction, then 'X is Y' is true") to the secondary inferences developed through rationalism and empiricism (like the coherence test), reason provides our most viable and valuable means of confirmation. Furthermore, in order to confirm any given assertion, we must employ deductive logic, for each of the inferences used in the seven different forms of confirmation is itself a deduction (for example, "My intuited assertions are often true; because the assertion 'A is B' was intuited, I can conclude that 'A is B' is true"). Each of the other forms of confirmation also relies substantially on induction to support the major premises of those inferences (e.g., "My intuited assertions about this kind of thing are often true"); because a principal reason we believe that they are valuable means for confirming truth is the fact that, on many occasions, they have done that in the past. Therefore, we need to recognize the dual and dominant role of reason in the confirmation of truth: not only is it a source of and means for confirming many specific assertions, but it is also the method through which we are able to apply, and to some extent, the basis upon which we are willing to apply, the other forms of confirmation in our searches for truth. Most of the limitations on reason (such as its utilization of unproven assumptions or its being subject to the limitations of language) are also shared by all of the other forms of confirmation, but its productivity regularly exceeds that of the other forms of confirmation. Reason is our primary method of disconfirmation as well, which is a tremendously important function in the search for truth. Finally, we should notice that, almost invariably, when two types of confirmation produce conflicting results and only one of those has rational support, we will take the rational side (although it may take us a while to accept it).

The two facets of logical reasoning are mutually interdependent: deduction must rely on induction for many of its premises, and induction must rely on deduction in order for its own observational premises to be productive. As Martin Johnson said, induction and deduction may be seen as different sides of a common scheme of thought.[39] Together they provide the bases for rational thought, which, felicitously, is inherent in the human mind.

4. INTUITION

Intuition is another form of confirmation which is supported inductively. We should all be able to recognize times in the past when we have become aware of assertions virtually instantaneously-from "out of the blue"-which have turned out to have been true. This is quite analogous to what happens with the recognition of present perception, only here it involves the recognition of present assertions which deal with a variety of other topics. Over time, repeated successes become a reason for believing in the truth of new assertions which appear to have been produced in the same manner.

Intuition as a means of confirming truth is also supported by external authority. We have many testimonies from others about the effectiveness of intuition as a path to truth (some of which were set out in Chapter 2). Studies by psychologists of our intuitive powers have provided authoritative support for its effectiveness from another perspective. In *Blink: The Power of Thinking Without Thinking*,[40] for example, Malcolm Gladwell reported on findings in that field concerning the validity and power of intuitive thinking.

Particular intuitive assertions can often be otherwise confirmed (and sometimes they stand in dire need of that). If intuitive insights are seen as hypotheses, then they would regularly be subjected to further confirmation. William Gordon said that we have to judge a concept produced by intuition critically,[41] and Alejandro Korn wrote that for comparative certainty on specific intuitions, we must turn to other sources, like science.[42]

As suggested by these comments, intuition has significant limitations as a source of confirmation, and it is far from self-sufficient. We can be in error not only on the content of an intuition but also in the identification of its source-as having been intuitively gleaned. But such limitations do not negate the propriety of concluding that intuition can assist us in confirming truths, because-at least sometimes-the intuitive inference is supportive of the truth of its content due to its effectiveness in finding it. Recognizing its limits merely helps us keep intuitive confirmation in perspective.

5. EXTERNAL AUTHORITY

We accept external authority as confirmation for several reasons. The first of these is necessity. As infants and children, we learned truths primarily from trusted external authorities-parents, other adults, older siblings, and so on. We should be able to recognize, in retrospect, that, without them, we would still be far from possessing many of the truths and understandings that we now have.[43] In addition, using external authority for confirmation is necessary because, for some kinds of assertions (such as those dealing with ancient history or with highly complex scientific research in a field with which we are unfamiliar), it is the only accessible form of confirmation. I have no other effective way of knowing about Julius Caesar or about the composition of moon rocks. Its comprehensiveness has been an additional reason for its general acceptance. Using external authorities greatly expands the number and types of assertions which we can, relatively reliably, accept as being true and which, therefore, turn out to be useful to us. The ease with which external authority can be employed, compared with other forms of confirmation, is another reason it is widely used. The time and energy that we usually expend in obtaining confirmation in this manner are relatively minimal: we can just ask or look it up. External authorities can also play important roles in the confirmation of many, if not most, of the assertions which we may have tentatively accepted through our personal applications of other forms of confirmation, because someone other than ourselves can provide helpful input on almost everything that happens to us.

However, we consider external authority to be a valid means of confirmation primarily due to the inductive support which exists for it. Because carefully selected external authorities have proven to be correct in a significant number of cases in the past, we believe that we can accept their input–in appropriate situations–as confirmation of truth in the present and in the future.[44] We have particularly found that the common assent of others in whom we have confidence strongly supports the truth of the statement under consideration. Indeed, it has been said that truth needs to be grounded in common or social assent,[45] which we obtain by referring to others who can make meaningful observations about a given assertion.

The relationship between external authority and the confirmation of truth has not generated as large a body of philosophical literature as may be found for some of the other approaches to the confirmation of truth.[46] However, in *Appeal to Expert Opinion: Arguments From Authority*, Douglas Walton provides a comprehensive review of this subject.[47] It is also addressed to a certain extent in the field of the sociology of knowledge. Emile Durkheim wrote that "A collective representation, because it is collective, already presents assurances of objectivity . . . (because) if it was in disagreement with the nature of things, it would not have succeeded in acquiring broad and prolonged dominion over minds."[48]

Much more attention has been devoted to appeals to external authority for the confirmation of truth in the area of revelation, which is the receipt of knowledge from an outside, independent source which is divine.[49] Revelation occurs either when our minds receive such truths directly (as if they were implanted) or when we perceive truths as they have become revealed in the external world (for historical examples, through trials by fire and water).

There are, of course, significant problems in using external authority as a means of confirmation. Because most external authorities are at least sometimes more interested in advancing their own personal agendas than in communicating the unvarnished truth, their credibility is thereby affected-especially when they offer opinions on assertions in which they have important stakes. In other words, in addition to sometimes being in error, other people may lie or shade the truth (either intentionally or unintentionally) for personal reasons. When we rely on an external authority, we obtain all of the consequences of that authority's errors, as well as the benefits from its truths. Furthermore, competing external authorities abound, so it can often be difficult for us to choose which ones (if any) we should accept. When we decide to consider a particular external authority to be trustworthy, we may not be making our selections rationally (which here primarily means inductively), but rather we may be relying on such factors as emotional ties or propinquity. It usually helps if the expert we are considering is in general agreement with other experts in that field; but that is not always the case, for there was a time when all expert physicists believed that a substance that they called "ether" existed throughout space, a conclusion which was effectively disconfirmed early in the twentieth century. William James, calling an assertion's origin "too obviously insufficient" as a test of truth, preferred instead to place credence in an assertion's "fruits" alone.[50] Finally, with regard to superhuman external authorities, as C. S. Peirce noted, it is difficult to know whether any given revelation is indeed inspired; and even if it is, it could be distorted or incomprehensible by the time it reaches us.[51] In other words, communications problems with all kinds of external authorities may abound, and these issues, to some extent, compromise their utility in the confirmation of truth.

Nonetheless, we continue to look to those who appear to know as much or more than we do about certain types of assertions for their guidance on those issues, and we often accept as true what they tell us is true because they say it is true. We do not have the time, resources, energy, or ability to perform confirmations by ourselves of all of the assertions about which we need to draw conclusions, even if we were so inclined. Furthermore, we could never "wipe the slate clean" and abandon all the things that we have already accepted as being true because of their confirmation by external authorities. Fortunately, we also have positive reasons for accepting and using external authority as a means of confirmation, as long as we take reasonable precautions and try to keep its problems-and its limitations-in perspective.

6. FAITH

We accept faith as confirmation for several reasons. First, it is inherent in our mental processes and critical to our ability to accept other forms of confirmation. As Augustine put it in this sense, "Believe that thou may understand."[52] Teilhard de Chardin thought verification of the legitimacy of faith resulted by descending "step by step, to ever more elementary beliefs, until I reach a certain fundamental intuition below which I can no longer distinguish anything at all."[53] A second justification of faith is the now-familiar inductive one: many people find that assertions originally believed because of faith are later supported by subsequent events, causing their acceptance of faith as a valid method of confirmation to become reinforced. Finally, it is argued that faith is justified on the ground that it is the only way to approach "real" or "higher" truths. Agreeing with other extreme fideists, Francois de La Mothe Le Vayer, for instance, said that "The Christian sceptic leaves his doubts at the foot of the altar, and accepts what Faith obligates him to believe."[54] Soren Kierkegaard saw faith as the only way to reach beyond the limits of reason, and he considered faith to be necessary in order to reach higher truths, saying that "Essential truths . . . must be apprehended via passionate choice . . . rather than abstract reflection."[55] Nicholas Berdyaev said that faith alone can provide us with the "higher" truth of "transcendental man."[56]

On faith we could accept any assertion; but in practice, we tend to accept only some assertions but not others. We also recognize that, on occasion, assertions which have been based on faith have been invalidated by subsequent contrary proofs. Not infrequently, reason, present perception, or external authority will disconfirm an assertion which previously had been accepted (or at least strongly urged) in large part through faith. A classic example of this outcome occurred with the Copernican explanation of the solar system.

While an assertion accepted on faith cannot-by definition-otherwise be fully confirmed, assertions accepted in part on faith are more likely to be true if they are also strongly supported by other forms of validation. As some have suggested, we test assertions of faith against life.[57] William James put it another way:

> In the history of Christian mysticism the problem how to discriminate between such messages and experiences as were really divine miracles, and such others as the demon in his malice was able to counterfeit . . . has always been a difficult one to solve. . . . In the end it had to come to our empiricist criterion: By their fruits ye shall know them, not by their roots. . . . No appearances whatever are infallible proofs of grace.[58]

John Erskine summarized the process involved in the selection of which assertions should be accepted on faith as follows: "The faith that needs the fewest altars, the hypothesis that leaves the least unexplained, survives."[59]

Being able to accept assertions on faith raises some problems in addition to the practical difficulty of determining which specific statements should be so accepted. One such problem is its own incomplete proof. Faith cannot be proven by or through itself, and its external supports are not completely sufficient, either. To a certain extent then, we are accepting faith on faith. Thus, we must necessarily rely on it for part of its own support (just as we have had to do for several of the other types of truth confirmations).

Some people, like Brand Blanshard, believe that faith cannot serve as a means for confirmation of truth because, if the grounds of belief are noncommunicable, they cannot be supportive of it.[60] That criticism, however, fails to recognize that we find truth support in other similarly noncommunicable ways (such as in intuition). In addition, to some extent the grounds for belief through faith or intuition *are* communicable: "I believe in the truth of Assertion 'X is Y' because I have faith in it or because I intuited it" is a cleanly conveyed and perfectly understandable assertion.

Notwithstanding its drawbacks, faith is a necessary component in the process of the confirmation of factual truth. The question is not whether we should accept confirmations of assertions based on faith. Rather, the questions are which assertions should be accepted in that manner, and how and to what extent should they be so accepted.

7. INTENTION

The first question here, once again, is whether any real confirmation is produced by an inference based upon intention. It would be unwise to underestimate the power of desire to affect future events, however. It is this power which generates the limited potential of intention as confirmation. Sometimes, when we strongly want an object or event to correspond to an assertion about its occurrence, we are able to affect that object or event so that it will come into agreement with the assertion. Knowing that we can make some dreams come true by hoping for them and then working diligently toward that hope, we can even find some inductive support for the use of wishes as validation of statements about the future. Because intentions made in the past have inspired us to undertake the activities necessary to make some predictions come true, we find justifiable support for believing that a new, similar intentional assertion will prove to be true as well.

One of the main problems with intention in this role is that the number of objects or events which we can affect in this manner is not very large. Most often, there is no necessary correlation between our self-directed activities and an assertion's truth; indeed, desire may even become a major impediment to the discovery of truth. George Boas, for example, said that when the pleasing, comforting wish is held to be truth, the result is logical hedonism, which is meaningless and inconsistent.[61]

However, because assertions about our personal futures may become self-fulfilling prophecies if they are susceptible to our actions, and therefore our desired objectives may become a real factor in determining whether a particular assertion will turn out to have been true, intention does constitute a valid form of confirmation. Our principal task whenever using intention as confirmation is to remember its extremely narrow parameters: it does no good (in terms of confirmation) to entertain intentions about the past or to intend to affect present or future events which are beyond our reach. But if I desire to have rice for dinner, it will usually come to pass in response to intentional activity on my part aimed at achieving that goal. "I will have rice for dinner" will often turn out to be a true statement because I wanted to have it, and I was justified in believing that statement was true when it was made on the basis of the reasonable assurance that I had in its likely verification by later events.

I have discussed seven different types of confirmation which we may use to support conclusions about the truth or falsity of assertions. Since categorizations are subjective creations, similar lists could contain more or fewer of them (e.g., a limited number of people would also include ESP) or could characterize them differently (e.g., using "testimony" rather than "external authority"). The list presented here is merely one way to describe the different manners in which we are able to verify truth; for, as the Islamic philosopher Averroes wrote more than eight centuries ago, there are several modes of access to but one truth.[62]

These seven means of confirmation are part of the framework to which we can refer and upon which we can rely in our efforts to verify factual truth. They provide a comprehensive approach because these seven forms reflect the different major kinds of foundations which our minds utilize for the inferential processes employed in these efforts. In addition, they are convenient ways in which to describe and discuss the different manners in which we confirm factual truth and to understand why certain statements are true and others are not true.

NOTES

1. Bertrand Russell, *The Analysis of Mind* (London: Allen & Urwin, 1971), p. 162.
2. John L. Pollock and Joseph Cruz, *Contemporary Theories of Knowledge*, 2nd ed. (Lanham, MD: Rowman & Littlefield, 1999), pp. 46–58.
3. Ludwig Wittgenstein, "Logic and Meaning," *Readings in Contemporary Philosophy*, p. 410.
4. W. V. Quine, *Philosophy of Logic* (Englewood Cliffs, NJ: Prentice Hall, 1970), p. 102.
5. William Werkmeister, *The Basis and Structure of Knowledge* (New York: Greenwood Press, 1968), p. 132.
6. Josiah Royce, *William James and Other Essays on the Philosophy of Life* (New York; Macmillan, 1911), p. 244.
7. Hans Reichenbach, "Predictive Knowledge," *Readings in Contemporary Philosophy*, p. 375.
8. Francis H. Parker and Henry B. Veatch, *Logic as a Human Instrument* (New York: Harper & Brothers, 1959), p. 285.
9. P. W. Bridgman, *The Ways Things Are* (Harvard University Press, 1959), p. 6.
10. Ibid., p. 115.
11. Causation has theoretical as well as practical problems. The former have been subjects of philosophical doubt, as discussed by Hume, among others. The latter derive principally from the complexity of the world and from difficulties in distinguishing real from merely apparent causes. See, e.g., Richard Taylor, "Causation," *The Encyclopedia of Philosophy*, vol. 2, pp. 56–66.
12. C. S. Peirce, "Notes on Scientific Philosophy," *Basic Problems of Philosophy*, p. 247.
13. Jose Ortega y Gasset, *The Origin of Philosophy* (New York: W. W. Norton & Co., 1967), p. 72.
14. H. P. Rickman, "Wilhelm Dilthey," *The Encyclopedia of Philosophy*, vol. 2, p. 406.
15. David D. Stern, *Wittgenstein on Mind and Language* (Oxford University Press, 1995), pp. 183–184.
16. Howard Isham, "Wilhelm von Humboldt," *The Encyclopedia of Philosophy*, vol. 4, p. 73.
17. Henri Poincare, "Science and Hypothesis," *Basic Problems of Philosophy*, p. 239.
18. According to Jean Piaget, the three principal factors involved in intellectual structure formation are "the maturation of the nervous system, experience acquired in interaction with the physical environment, and the influence of the social milieu."

Barbel Inhelder and Jean Piaget, *The Growth of Logical Thinking*, Anne Parsons, et al., trans. (New York, Basic Books, 1958), p. 138. As social factors, P. G. Richmond, in *An Introduction to Piaget* (New York: Basic Books, 1971), p. 83, cited language, beliefs and values, forms of reasoning accepted as valid, and kinds of relationships between members of a given society.

19. See, e.g., Steve Fuller, *Social Epistemology*, 2nd ed. (Bloomington, IN: Indiana University Press, 2002), pp. 4, 91.

20. Immanuel Kant, *Critique of Pure Reason*, Werner S. Pluhar, trans. (Indianapolis, IN: Hackett Publishing Co., 1996), p. 458.

21. Sarvepalli Radhakrishnan, et al., *A Source Book in Indian Philosophy* (Princeton University Press, 1957), p. 353.

22. Werner Stark, ed., *Of Learned Ignorance* (Yale University Press, 1954), p. 12.

23. Bridgman, *The Way Things Are*, p. 6.

24. Richard H. Popkin, *The History of Scepticism From Erasmus to Spinoza* (University of California Press, Berkeley, 1979), pp. 3–4.

25. Durant, *The Mansions of Philosophy*, pp. 26–27.

26. Rogers, *What Is Truth?*, p. 28.

27. Blanshard, *The Nature of Thought*, vol. 1, p. 374.

28. Bertrand Russell, *Philosophical Essays* (New York: Simon and Schuster, 1966), p. 95. Rescher also pointed out the equivocation among the conceptions of "working out" or "positive effects" or "utilities." Rescher, *The Coherence Theory of Truth*, p. 164.

29. Gertrude Ezorsky, "Pragmatic Theory of Truth," *The Encyclopedia of Philosophy*, vol. 6, p. 428.

30. George Santayana, *Realms of Being* (New York: Charles Scribner's Sons, 1942), p. 449.

31. J. L. Mackie, *Truth, Probability and Paradox: Studies in Philosophical Logic* (Oxford: Clarendon Press, 1973), p. 25.

32. See Chapter 1 and Chapter 4 for further elaboration of these points.

33. Hans Reichenbach, *Experience and Prediction* (University of Chicago Press, 1938), p. 350.

34. Ibid., p. 351.

35. Royce, *William James*, p. 220.

36. G. A. Rauche, *Contemporary Philosophical Alternatives and the Crisis of Truth: A Critical Study of Positivism, Existentialism, and Marxism* (The Hague: Martinus Nijhoff, 1970), p. 20.

37. Karl A. Popper, *Conjectures and Refutations: Growth of Scientific Knowledge* (New York: Basic Books, 1962), p. 29.

38. Solomon Diamond, *The World of Probability: Statistics in Science* (New York: Basic Books, 1964), p. 177.

39. Johnson, *Science and the Meaning of Truth*, p. 47.

40. Malcolm Gladwell, *Blink: The Power of Thinking Without Thinking* (Boston: Little, Brown and Company, 2005).

41. Gordon, *Synectics*, p. 156.

42. Arthur Berndtson, "Alejandro Korn," *The Encyclopedia of Philosophy*, vol. 4, p. 360.

43. As one example, Aristotle, in *Nichomachean Ethics*, 1144b, wrote that if we do not have a guide in morals, we stumble.

44. See, e.g., Richard T. De George, *The Nature and Limits of Authority* (Lawrence, KS: University Press of Kansas, 1985); and E. D. Watt, *Authority* (New York: St. Martin's Press, 1982).

45. See, e.g., Jurgen Habermas, *Moral Consciousness and Communicative Action*, Christian Lenbardt and Shierry W. Nicholsen, trans. (The MIT Press, 1990); and Werner Stark, *The Sociology of Knowledge* (London: Routledge & Kegan Paul, 1958), p. 336.

46. It has, nonetheless, long been considered. See, for example, George Santayana, *Dominations and Powers* (New York: C. Scribner's Sons, 1951).

47. Douglas Walton, *Appeal to Expert Opinion: Arguments From Authority* (University Park, PA: Pennsylvania State University Press, 1997).

48. Emile Durkheim, *The Elementary Forms of Religious Life*, Karen E. Fields, trans. (New York: The Free Press, 1995), p. 439.

49. Many have said that truth comes from God, and this is often considered to be a basic tenet of Christian belief. See, e.g., E. F. Osborn, "Clement of Alexandria," *The Encyclopedia of Philosophy*, vol. 2, p. 122.

50. William James, *The Varieties of Religious Experience* (London: Longmans, Green & Co., 1941), pp. 19–20.

51. Peirce, "Notes on Scientific Philosophy," pp. 251–252.

52. Augustine, *Tractate* 29, Ch. 1, 6.

53. Teilhard de Chardin, *How I Believe*, p. 15.

54. Popkin, *The History of Scepticism*, p. 96.

55. *The Cambridge Companion to Kierkegaard*, Alastair Hanney and Gordon D. Marino, eds. (Cambridge University Press, 1998), p. 247.

56. Nicholas Berdyaev, *Truth and Revelation*, R. M. French, trans. (New York: Collier Books, 1962), p. 26.

57. See, e.g., Teilhard de Chardin, *How I Believe*, p. 15.

58. James, *The Varieties of Religious Experience*, pp. 19–20.

59. John Erskine, 'The Moral Obligation to Be Intelligent," *Gateway to the Great Books*, p. 13.

60. Blanshard, *The Nature of Thought*, vol. 2, pp. 222–224.

61. George Boas, *The History of Ideas* (New York: Charles Scribner's Sons, 1969), p. 193.

62. Stuart MacClintock, "Averroes," *The Encyclopedia of Philosophy*, vol. 1, p. 223.

Chapter Four

Confirmation and Certainty

For centuries, the issue of certainty has served as a philosophical touchstone to separate epistemological optimists from epistemological pessimists. The optimists are exemplified by George Santayana, who said that there simply must be absolute certainty, and if we did not have absolute truth, we would invent it.[1] The pessimists may perhaps be represented best by Xenophanes, who said that all human knowledge is guesswork.[2]

Certainty, if it is possible, is indeed a prize. It provides tremendous psychological strength to those who believe that they have it.[3] It also has remarkable generative powers; for once we have a certain truth, it can beget scores of derivative truths. Pascal contended that we discover new truths only when they are based upon secure foundation.[4] Other philosophers have employed this method to create elaborate metaphysical and epistemological systems derived from their certain "first truths."

One might expect certainty to be a fairly simple matter. After all, if something is certain, is it not absolutely and indubitably true? But things relating to truth are rarely as simple as they could be; and neither is certainty, because we identify and utilize many different degrees of assurance when we discuss truth.

1. THE ACCESSIBILITY OF ABSOLUTE CERTAINTY

The ultimate form of certainty that could possibly be achieved is absolute certainty, which is clearly distinguishable from all other less-exacting forms of it. Absolute certainty may be positively defined as a complete and total confirmation in which all the conceivable support in favor of an assertion's truth has been obtained. Negatively defined, an assertion is absolutely certain if it is completely indubitable (i.e., if no doubt about its truth is even possible). Both the positive and negative criteria need to be met before a confirmed assertion should be called "absolutely certain," because to fail to do so could, at the very least, lead to some doubt about it at one end of the inquiry or the other. Consequently, if absolute certainty can occur, that assertion's truth must be fixed and incorrigible: it would be definitely known, and it could not possibly be in error.

When we discuss whether absolute certainty is possible, we are also considering whether there are any limits to our ability to confirm the truth of an assertion. We can achieve absolute certainty about an assertion only if there are no limits on its confirmation; for if we cannot obtain all conceivable support and eliminate all conceivable doubt, those limitations would prevent us from concluding that we have reached absolute certainty. The possibility of absolute certainty thus varies directly with the potential for the unlimited confirmation of truth.

Can we obtain absolute certainty? I have read arguments supporting an affirmative response to this question by proponents of five of the different forms of confirmation. The two forms without such champions are memory and intention. Memory is generally considered suspect in this role because of the recurring proofs of the regularity of its errors (e.g., "Where did I leave my keys?"), so it simply does not belong anywhere near absolute incorrigibility. Neither does intention, which, in the first place, barely rises to the level of confirmation and then does so only in highly limited circumstances. In addition, because intention pertains to statements about the future (even near-term intentions, like "I will get a drink of water"), and because the future cannot be fully known ahead of time, confirmation by this method could never hope to banish all conceivable doubts about such a statement, let alone provide complete support for the truth of any such assertion.

The other five forms of confirmation, however, each have ardent supporters on the question of certainty. They all need to be examined more closely, first to ascertain whether any of them-in and of itself-can provide us with absolute certainty about the truth of an assertion.

Present perception has often been discussed as a possible source of absolute certainty. Some philosophers ascribe that quality to present sense perceptions, while others find it in the awareness of certain present mental states or thoughts.

Turning first to present sense perceptions, Ernst Mach wrote that he cannot be wrong if he is asserting that he is having various sensations: No one is in a position to dispute it, and he "cannot be mistaken about it."[5] Indeed, it has been strenuously argued that "basic" propositions or statements, which are limited to assertions about things which are directly provided through the senses-the "this here"–are indeed incorrigible.[6] We can, of course, always be wrong about the recognition of specific sense perceptions at the higher levels of their interpretations. To say, "It is true, that is a bluebird" entails a judgment about our perceptions of certain sensations that we are having; but that judgment could be in error on the interpretive level because, for example, it could be a fake bluebird or it could be a bluejay. Arguments like Mach's, however, refer to more fundamental stuff-to sensations at a point supposedly prior to our interpretations of them. To say "that blue space above" rather than "sky" only begins to indicate the direction these philosophers intend to move perceptions of basic sensations away from the normal meaning and context that we almost automatically supply to them.

As we move even further away from sensory error and interpretive doubt, however, could we ever be mistaken in making assertions that recognize our initial basic sensations (the things that precede our perceptual interpretations of them)? When we sense light or a sharp object, should we not be able to do so without potentially erroneous content from our interpretations about conditions in the external world? Could we *ever* be in error in reporting the perception of a sensation of light when we have that perception-regardless of whether our eyes are then sensing external light-or in reporting the perception of the sensation of touching a sharp object when we have that perception-regardless of whether we are actually touching anything at all? While whenever there is interpretation, there may be error, and while whenever context is relied upon, there may be error-and therefore assertions like "I see the sun shining" or "I feel a knife" cannot be matters of absolute certainty-perhaps the perception of a basic sensation of light or of a sharp object would avoid the potential errors which seem to prevent us from reaching absolute certainty on the higher interpretive levels. Even if there were no good reason for having a sensation of light or of feeling a sharp touch (i.e., even if no stimulus for those nerve impulses could be ascertained), that would not necessarily mean that such a sensation was not presently being felt and that we were not then sensing light or a sharp touch. Viewed so immediately, how could it possibly be wrong to assert that we are perceiving light if we are sensing light, even if we cannot discover any real cause for that sensation-or even if there is no "real" cause for that sensation?

While the immediacy of a conscious reaction to a sensation of recognizing light or to a sensation of being touched by a sharp object does greatly diminish the chance of interpretive error, when we search for absolute certainty, we must determine whether the statement has received all conceivable support and is completely indubitable. First of all, however, I do not believe that we can assert anything nearly as "basic" as some of these proponents suggest, for we are always able to discern some level of interpretation at work; and where there is interpretation, there is always opportunity for error. As William Werkmeister wrote, basic statements "go beyond mere datum and brute fact and become enmeshed in context of meaning and thought which give it significance."[7] If this is so, then interpretive and definitional error re-emerge as possibilities even with regard to assertions about the most basic sensations and perceptions of sensations, and that constitutes one reason why this type of statement cannot be considered to be absolutely certain. In addition, as Karl Popper noted, any basic statement may be subjected to further tests, and to that process there would be no natural end.[8] We can always take a closer look or touch something again (and again) (and again) or in a different way; so all conceivable support for the truth of such an assertion could never be achieved. Furthermore, when we formulate an assertion about the perception of a sensation, that takes time. Anything that takes time involves memory, and whenever memory is involved, error may occur. An assertion takes seconds (or at least milliseconds); and, by the time the assertion is finished, the involvement of our irrefutably fallible memories undermines any contention of *absolutely* incorrigible truth for any assertion we may care to make about basic sensations. Assertions are never instantaneous, so absolute certainty cannot reside in any of those purporting to report on "present" sense perceptions. Finally, one of the means which we may use for further testing of assertions about sensations and perceptions is external authority. We can obtain feedback from others on the truth or falsity of many such assertions, and we may find ourselves entertaining doubts even about basic statements when we receive conflicting information about them from a reliable source. A different opinion about the matter can certainly diminish our confidence in the truth of an assertion, even if it is only about a basic sensation. For example, "Nothing sharp is now touching your back" can make our assertion to the contrary dubitable. And we can almost always consult one or more external authorities on such matters.

An assertion which is based upon the recognition of a perception of a basic physical sensation should not be considered to be incorrigible for one additional set of reasons. Any given experience with sensations does not necessarily preclude the possibility of illusions, dreams, hallucinations, mirages, hypnosis, wishful thinking, psychological or physical impairments, evil demons, or brain-in-a-vat arguments. Thus, even the assertion "that blue space above" may be false because, for example, I may be dreaming about seeing a blue space rather than actually seeing one.

Because of the possibilities of interpretive error in statements about our sensations, because of the necessary use of other fallible means in the confirmation of assertions about present sensory perceptions, because of the regular availability of additional confirmations for them, and because of the possibilities of illusions, dreams, and other similar problems, this means of confirming truth–at least when it is considered by itself-fails to satisfy our quest for absolute certainty. Such assertions will not have all possible support for their truth, and some degree of doubt about them will always be possible.

Because present perception as a means deals not only with physical sensations but also with mental states and thoughts (e.g., "I am feeling sad"), the possibility of obtaining absolute certainty for this second type of present perception must also be examined. T. H. Huxley, for one, thought that we can achieve certain knowledge in assertions about our mental phenomena or states of consciousness,[9] which include, for example, the recognition of joy or sadness. When we are feeling joyful, can we not say for sure that we are feeling joyful?

Once again, however, we encounter the possibilities of illusions, dreams, hallucinations, and other conceivable sources of error in our perceptions (e.g., am I really sad if I am only dreaming about being sad?). In addition, most of our assertions about particular states or conditions of consciousness (like "I am happy") involve meanings and interpretations. Any time we formulate assertions about such feelings or mental states, we engage in a level of understanding which may be susceptible to interpretive mistake, as well. While "It is true that I feel happy" is indeed true when I feel happy, I may be thinking or saying that when I am simply mistaken about happiness itself or when I am deluding myself about my feelings for one reason or another. The possibility of interpretive errors is demonstrated by the meaningfulness of such statements as "I thought I was happy *then*, but now I can see that I really wasn't." We should also recognize the continual possibility of further testing, as well as the inherent limitations due to the involvement of memory. Therefore, because of the same kinds of problems which are encountered with assertions about present physical sensations, we are not able to find complete confirmability for, or complete indubitability in, assertions about our recognitions of awe or joy or sadness or any other internal mental state.

One particular type of assertion about present mental perceptions which deserves further scrutiny in any discussion about absolute certainty deals with our awareness of our own consciousness, which has been called the paradigm of certain knowledge. Descartes considered his knowledge of his mind's existence to be indubitably certain. Many others have agreed with him, including William James, who said that the only certain truth is that the present phenomenon of consciousness exists.[10]

While I believe that it is true that "My present consciousness exists" when I am thinking about it, even this type of assertion does not meet the requirements for absolute certainty. The present question is whether a single form of confirmation can be used to verify that a truth is absolutely certain. We must, however, use other forms of confirmation-in addition to present mental perception-to support this type of assertion (including reason, for example). Each of these assertions also will have internal and external antecedents which, upon examination, may not themselves be as strongly supported as the assertion itself appears to be. For example, what is "consciousness"? What does it mean for something to "exist"? These concepts must be understood and accepted before we can confirm that this assertion is meaningful, and then whether it is correct, let alone certain; and we can always have definitional or interpretive error with any word or concept which is involved in such an assertion. Even reduced versions of Descartes' "foundational" assertion which have been designed to avoid some of these issues (e.g., "Thinking is taking place; therefore, there must be that which thinks"[11]) have the same kind of antecedent issues (a previous understanding of words like "think" and "thinking" and of logic and language). Therefore, not even the confidence which we can have in assertions about our own consciousness provided by our present perception of it-at least by itself-raises such statements to the level of absolute certainty.

Intuition has also been promoted as a means of achieving absolute certainty. Bergson believed that absolutes are possible only within an intuition,[12] while phenomenologists argued that certain knowledge can be obtained through the immediate "intuition of essences."[13]

Intuition fails to meet either criterion for absolute certainty, however. One problem is that we may always have misidentified something as an intuition. We should recall that the primary support for intuition as a means of confirmation is systemic: we trust particular intuitions because we have found intuition to be a reasonably dependable source of truth. Occasionally, intuitions turn out to be warmed-over ideas from external authorities whose input was forgotten long ago, however. If we have gotten the source of the assertion wrong, then it is not and cannot be confirmed by intuition at all. Furthermore, while we may feel sure that we intuit some assertions that simply cannot be wrong, our sense of confidence is not foolproof. Some of my intuitions have in the past proven to have been wrong, and from what I have read and heard, this has happened to many others, as well. Because intuition by itself provides no sure way to distinguish between true intuitions and false intuitions, other forms of confirmation should always be employed to help validate the truth or uncover the falsity of an intuited assertion. We thus must continually recognize the possibility of error in intuitions, for they are sometimes subsequently disconfirmed by information provided through one or more of the other forms of confirmation. We therefore cannot banish all conceivable doubt that an intuition may be in error when its confirmation is limited to intuition alone, and we cannot provide all conceivable support for an intuited assertion merely by resorting to intuition by itself.

Turning next to reason, it should not take long to dismiss induction as a possible route to absolute certainty. Inductive logic has never attracted many claims of any kind of certainty, let alone absolute certainty.[14] On the one hand, we do not acquire all the conceivable support for any assertion inductively to the extent that it is predictive. Inductive conclusions based upon a sampling propose that the conclusion will apply to the unsampled members; but that would still remain to be seen until all members of that class were tested. Nothing about the future can be considered *absolutely* certain because there is always a chance that it will turn out differently than anticipated (even though that might require an extraordinary change or intervention). Inductive assertions are not indubitable because, as noted by Pierre Gassandi, among others, "it is always possible that a negative instance may turn up later."[15] Furthermore, some degree of doubt exists about several of the bases of induction, including not only the present sense perceptions which provide most of the data used in inductions but also the underlying principle of the uniformity of nature.[16] We can safely conclude, therefore, that the inductive side of rational verification is incapable of producing either total confirmation or complete indubitability.

Deductive logic is, however, quite another matter. It has been held out both as an example and as a means of obtaining absolute truth since the time of Aristotle.[17] Some of the truths of deductive logic may even be tautological, which, stated another way, means that those things which we have created as equivalencies are equivalent. Absent any internal error-which should be apparent, or at least discoverable, upon careful review-tautological assertions (like "A bachelor is an unmarried man") and assertions reflecting several of the most basic rules of deduction (which are employed, for example, in statements like "It is true either that this string of words is a sentence or that it is not a sentence") *must* be true. Indeed, the law of noncontradiction has been deduction's most popular warrior in this regard because of its alleged indubitability and its purported ability to "defeat the total skeptic." Finally, as could also be expected, mathematical truths (which are clearly related to deductive logic) are also often raised as a standard of absolute certainty. George Boas, for instance, said that only in math has invariable truth been obtained.[18]

The problem with acceding to these claims is that, while they may have obtained the best possible support that we have been able to find for their truth, assertions of deductive logic are still not able to attain absolute certainty because they do not and will not have all conceivable support for their truth. While we may feel certain about deductive truths, as Pyrrho noted, each deduction always begs the question about the truth of its conclusion because it only *assumes* the truth of its premises.[19] With any given deduction, we may reasonably ask for more support for-and thus may entertain some doubt about-the conclusion on the grounds that the premises ultimately rest (to at least some extent) upon unproven assumptions. Second, deductive logic may sometimes be misapplied, so that type of potential error also exists within every deduction that we make. Third, any deductive or mathematical system being used cannot be logically proven only through itself (see Godel's theorem, which holds that such a formal system cannot be proven within that system[20]). Consequently, we must entertain some systemic doubt about them, which is an additional impediment to achieving absolute certainty through such a means. Finally, all of the truth of a deduction stands only as true as its context-as true as the system, language, and meaning which give it life. To the extent that the truth of any given deductive assertion is relative to the truth of other assertions and principles, it becomes uncertain to the same extent that those other assertions and principles are or may be uncertain. Werkmeister wrote that even the truth of a proposition that "The shortest distance between two points is a straight line" is dependent upon a relative geometrical system.[21] This relativism, which is a fundamental characteristic of deductive logic and of mathematics, is inconsistent with absolute certainty. For that reason, and because of the assumed nature of deductive premises, the potential for logical error, and the lack of internal logical proofs for it, deductive reason cannot achieve absolute certainty by itself alone.

Turning next to external authority, I have not found any credible argument that supports the theory that one or more *human* external authorities are, by themselves, capable of providing absolute certainty for any specific truth. Furthermore, uniformity of belief offers no assurance of complete certainty. Even if all of the available human external authorities were to produce exactly the same report about an assertion, to be human is-as has been and is continually being proven-to be capable of error. As Abraham Lincoln said, "You can fool all of the people some of the time." We must therefore doubt-to some degree-all external authorities who are human, both when considered singly and when considered collectively. Because of this constant possibility of error, we cannot ascribe to another person or to any group of persons the capacity to bestow incorrigible certainty upon any given assertion.

The more compelling arguments in favor of obtaining absolute certainty through external authority are those which assert that it can be acquired through divine revelation. While divine beings could be capable of perfect knowledge of truth and of absolute certainty, this treatise is on the nature and extent of human knowledge of truth. One problem with our human knowledge in this context is that even revelations to us from a divine being must be received by and filtered through our human minds, which may not only color and distort them but also may have difficulty in distinguishing true revelations from false ones (or from dreams or hallucinations). Other problems for us occur in distinguishing among competing revelations or in evaluating revelations challenged by other data. In such cases, we often are able to refer to other forms of confirmation. Therefore, a confirmation based upon revelation by a divine external authority alone will probably not be fully completed. Given the potential errors in communication and given contradictions in the sources and data, at least some degree of legitimate doubt about specific divine revelations which are or have been conveyed to and through humans remains possible. While some people are nevertheless still willing to ascribe absolute certainty to statements by a few individuals who occupy certain high religious positions (like the Pope or the Dalai Lama), and while many others believe that these individuals directly communicate with and receive absolutely certain truths from the spiritual world, both of those beliefs are grounded in faith, which has its own problems in this area, as will be discussed next. In addition, I suspect that every pope and dalai lama would admit to having made errors about some assertions in the past and to being capable of making some types of errors again, as well.

Finally, with regard to the five different kinds of confirmation which arguably may lead in a straight path to absolute certainty, a number of people believe that at least some assertions which are founded on faith are absolutely certain. If any assertion is believed strongly enough-like the primary tenets of organized religions are believed by many-it is natural also to characterize its certainty as being beyond doubt because the believer has none (and wants none).

A number of problems exist with the contention that faith alone can produce absolute certainty, however. As with intuition, it is sometimes difficult to identify faith as the real basis for the truth of an assertion. As with intuition, faith only serves as a validating inference for truth when it really is faith that causes the firm belief. If it is caused by something else, then we would need to analyze that something else in terms of the certainty of that belief. Thus, to the extent that we may be mistaken about faith as being the basis for our belief in an assertion (which should be recognized as a continual possibility), there is the chance of error in confirmation by faith. We should also recognize the effect of the fact that we had several high hurdles to cross in proposing that it is appropriate to accept faith as a means of confirming truth in the first place. The justifications we can identify which support faith as a valid form of confirmation are less than sure themselves, for induction, need, and the arguable transcendence of faith over reason are not the stuff of certainty. Finally, beliefs based on faith are at times contradictory or conflicting. Whenever we try to determine which of those assertions, if any, may be true, we resort to additional inferences based upon other forms of confirmation. Thus, support for the truth of an assertion based upon faith alone is often recognized even by some of its own adherents as being insufficient for this task.

Consequently, absolute certainty is not an accessible level of assurance for a confirmation established solely by means of faith. While we may attain a high degree of personal confidence in the certainty of an assertion through faith beyond which we are not interested in questioning, we do not reach the point where others who may be skeptical about the certainty of that assertion simply make no sense when they voice their objections to such a conclusion. Feeling completely sure of the truth of a statement is not the same thing as confirming absolute certainty. That truths are undoubted does not make them indubitable.

From the above analysis, I have to conclude that no single form of confirmation is able to produce absolute certainty about the truth of any assertion. The next question, however, is whether it might still be found by using several of the forms together. To examine this possibility, I will look at the extent of assurance gains which may be attained when we use combinations of means specifically in the context of several kinds of assertions which are among those most likely to be considered to be certain.

While I concluded that assertions about present sense perceptions could not be deemed to be absolutely certain based upon confirmation by their recognition alone, that may not be the case when we are also able to apply some of the other forms of confirmation in support of the truth of statements about our physical sensations. For example, the possibility of errors in sense perceptions due to interpretive problems or to illusions, dreams, hallucinations, and so forth may clearly be mitigated by consulting external authorities. We can ask a friend standing nearby whether she also heard something that we think we heard, and if she says that she did, that would increase the support we have found for the truth of that assertion. Deductive reason may also provide support for assertions about present sense perceptions, particularly on the higher interpretive levels (e.g., "Around here, a quail's song sounds like 'bob-white'; I hear a bird that looks like a quail singing 'bob-white'; therefore, I hear a quail."). But assistance from these additional forms of confirmation still fails to eliminate the types of problems which we always face in confirming our knowledge about external objects. In the above example, I could be dreaming not only about the sound, but also about my friend. I could also be mistaken on the higher interpretive levels (e.g., I may be hearing someone imitating the sound of a quail). These problems exist even for more basic interpretations of sense perceptions or sensations, like "Sounds I hear that I did not make are made by other people or things; I hear a sound I did not make; therefore, that sound was made by someone or something else." I may not, for example, have really heard a sound but only imagined it or was just "hearing things." While asking someone else to confirm an assertion about a sense perception may help, that reinforcement cannot dispel all lingering legitimate uncertainty, even if it may be fairly minuscule. The most basic sense data could be dreamt; and we cannot shore up the certainty of basic sense data by resorting to an external authority without again delving into the possibility of interpretive error in the external authority himself, herself, or itself, and without acknowledging the reliability issues raised by all such communications with external authorities. Finally, no external authority can offer much assistance when I assert an internal perception of a basic sensation because they do not have direct access to my mind's perceptions. If I see a light and assert that I see it, they cannot look inside my mind to witness what I am seeing. Therefore, even when we use external authorities and reason in combination with our recognition of present sense perceptions, we are unable to find absolute certainty in basic statements about sensations.

Present mental perceptions also warrant closer scrutiny as we try to determine whether the use of multiple forms of confirmation may lead to absolute certainty. Even here, however, we find that the potential misidentifications and errors in such statements as "It is true that I feel happy" are not made completely impossible by the most careful reasoning or by assistance from the most incisive external authorities for the same reasons that they are unable to do so for assertions about present sense perceptions. While the use of other forms of confirmation can increase our confidence in the truth of such an assertion, it cannot eliminate all conceivable doubts that we can possibly have about it.

As usual, one present mental assertion deserves more careful consideration-the Cartesian "I think, therefore I am," or in a related form, "It is true that I exist." However, the "antecedents" of these statements cannot be completely validated by present perception in combination with reason and external authority because their own internal limitations do not disappear when they happen to be performing supplementary roles. Those somewhat dubious antecedents include, generally, language, logic and meaning, and, specifically, the meanings of "I," "think," "therefore," and "am," and they remain somewhat dubious no matter how many external authorities we may consult (and we will never run out of them). Because none of our general systems of language or logic is susceptible to complete certainty, and because specific words in any given language are fluid and can be imprecise, the negative criterion for absolute certainty (complete indubitability) cannot be met with these assertions. The positive criterion will not be met, either, because further support for both the internal and external antecedents of these statements will always be conceivable. We can continue to ask questions about some of the foundational assumptions which we use to posit and understand them, and then we can delve further into the assumptions of those assumptions and their foundations, and so on.

Finally, the use of multiple forms of confirmation cannot sufficiently shore up the levels of certainty we can have in tautologies or in mathematical statements, either. Even though they are both strongly confirmed by deductive reason, these statements do not surmount their context merely by gaining additional support from, for example, external authorities or intuition. Context cannot be ignored, nor can it be exceeded. Even the facial indubitability of "It is true that $2 + 2 = 4$" and of "It is true that a bachelor is an unmarried man" is relative to the internal and external antecedents of those assertions, about which, as noted above, neither requirement of absolute certainty can be obtained.

In conclusion, a review of several of the more promising types of assertions reveals that even when we use multiple forms of confirmation together, absolute certainty is still not possible for us. Each form brings at least one Achilles heel into the mix that makes the result susceptible to conceivable doubt and/or open to continual search for additional meaningful support. Therefore, the use of all of the forms of confirmation together simply cannot completely secure the total confirmation of any true assertion.

My conclusion that absolute certainty is impossible for us to attain is, of course, relative to the definition which I have provided and used for it- namely, that to obtain it, we must meet the strictest demands of both its positive and negative criteria. It may be argued that, in so doing, I have stacked the deck; but I am of the opinion that *absolute* certainty should meet the most-stringent-possible requirements for it, or else it would not be absolute. I would also note that negative conclusions about the possibility of absolute certainty have been drawn by many diverse philosophers, from F. H. Bradley, who thought that to be absolute, truth would have to be outside of any frame of reference,[22] to John Dewey, who said that nothing we do can "give anything approaching absolute certitude"; we can find "insurance but no assurance."[23] C. S. Peirce wrote:

> There are three things to which we can never hope to attain by reasoning, namely, absolute certainty, absolute exactitude, absolute universality. We cannot be absolutely certain that our conclusions are even approximately true.... Even if we could ascertain with absolute certainty and exactness that the ratio of sinful men to all men was 1 to 1; still among the infinite generations of men there would be room for any finite number of sinless men without violating that proportion. The case is the same with a seven legged calf.[24]

2. DEGREES OF CERTAINTY AND ASSURANCE

Absolute certainty is not the only grail worth seeking, however. We have regular access to a number of other degrees of assurance in the truth of assertions, several even involving what we may appropriately call "lesser degrees of certainty." Because some confirmations of truths are much more successful than others, we are able to distinguish among varying levels of assurance that we may be able to reach for different truths. Therefore, once we decide that we may properly conclude that the truth of an assertion has been supported, we can proceed to determine where the results may lie along the continuum of assurance, which ranges from absolute certainty down through different degrees of lesser certainty and probability.[25]

When an assertion is both fully supported by all of the different types of potentially valid confirmation which are available to us with the exception of "systemic" limitations (those which involve problems with the justifications of the inferential forms or with language and logic themselves, as discussed above), and when the assertion is otherwise indubitable on its face and cannot be meaningfully disbelieved, we have what may be called "relative certainty" (and not, we should be careful to note and distinguish, an assertion that is "relatively certain"). The assurance we may have in the truth of a statement reaches the level of relative certainty when it has been confirmed by all of the potentially effective proofs that we have thought up and tried for it (other than those dealing with systemic limitations) and when no legitimate doubt (other than systemic doubts) exists about the truth of that particular assertion. Relative certainty accepts the limitations inherent in our means of confirmation and in our systems and means of thought, but it requires that everything else fall into place in support of the truth of that statement. This certainty is relative only to the necessary frames of reference that exist for every assertion; and thus, the relativity involved is essentially just recognized context.

Relative certainty is not only possible for us, but it is also routinely obtained by us. This degree of certainty is primarily limited, however, to things like fundamental deductive principles, tautologies, basic mathematical propositions, and statements about the present existence of consciousness. "It is true that "$2 + 2 = 4$" is certainly true, relative only to the mathematical system of which it is a part, to the accepted definitions of its terms, and to the limitations of the directly applicable forms of confirmation. The same analysis and conclusions apply to assertions about the present existence of consciousness (e.g., "I think, therefore I am"). Disbelief in the truth of these kinds of statements cannot be meaningfully asserted or maintained within the frames of reference which are provided for all human thought.

Slightly below relative certainty on the continuum of degrees of assurance about truth is what may be called "effective certainty" (but not, again, "effectively certain").[26] In addition to the doubts generated by systemic limitations (which are a given for all of these "lesser" degrees of assurance), limited doubts about a specific assertion may exist, and additional support for it may be conceivable, but it would still reach the level of effective certainty if we justifiably believe that the prospects for its disconfirmation are so remote that they should be discounted on that basis alone. For effective certainty, we should attain all the important available information about an assertion's truth, which should either be supportive of its truth or, for any contrary input, be clearly erroneous. The mere existence of dissent does not, of course, undermine a conclusion about the accuracy of a statement, because people disagree for not only good reasons (sometimes) but also for bad reasons (sometimes). While additional support for the assertion would be conceivable, that would need to appear to be highly likely to turn out to be repetitive or unimportant for some other reason. We should also have no reasonable doubt about the truth of such an assertion, so this level of assurance can be compared to the "beyond a reasonable doubt" standard established for determinations of guilt in criminal cases in our courts.

Among the major kinds of assertions about which we may at least sometimes reach effective certainty-given enough confirmation for a statement of this type-are those dealing with present physical sensations and present mental states (e.g., "It is true that I hear a telephone ringing" and "It is true that I miss you"), other statements about the present (e.g., "It is true that the Presidential candidates are now debating"), statements about the past (whether based on personal memory, like "It is true that I just saw the game," or based on reliable external authorities, like "It is true that Thomas Jefferson was President of the United States at the time of the Louisiana Purchase"), and assertions which have been produced through the scientific method (e.g., "It is true that water boils at 212 degrees Fahrenheit"). Indeed, at least some assertions in most of the different major types of statements that we make which have truth potential can reach effective certainty, thereby setting the standard for that class. Even some normative statements may attain this level of certainty, such as "It is true that murder is wrong and/or that one should not commit murder," or "It is true that some sunsets are beautiful."

Relative and effective certainty should succeed in satisfying most of our needs and desires for certitude. These levels give us strong assurance in the reliability of those truths, and they generate workable general premises (e.g., through inductive conclusions made about a series of sense perceptions or through tautologies like "A husband is a married man"). While no such assertion is absolutely incorrigible, we can still acquire a considerable amount of reliable knowledge through deductions made from premises which have reached these levels of certainty. The only caveat is that we have to carry over to the particular conclusions which we thereafter draw from such premises the limited doubts which are inherent in and recognized by them.

Beneath these two levels of certainty comes a range of probability. Some philosophers have believed that we must generally be content with the reasonable or probable. According to R. M. Chisholm, writing in an article about Sextus Empiricus, we can reach a reasonably high degree of probability for non-empirical assertions, but we can never reach absolute certainty.[27] James wrote, "If we claim only reasonable probability, it will be as much as men who love truth can ever at any given moment hope to have within their grasp."[28] Bertrand Russell also thought that most knowledge is only probable.[29]

Two major probability classes which may be distinguished along this continuum reflect relatively high degrees of assurance. The first of these applies to those assertions which are "highly probable," and the second applies to those assertions whose truth is "more probable than not." Statements which belong to a type which might sometimes produce assertions that reach the higher levels of relative or effective certainty but for some reason have failed to do so in those specific instances should be assigned to one of these probability categories (at best).

We say that the truth of an assertion is "highly probable" when we may have some doubts about it but none of those doubts is definitive and any other doubts have been substantially countered, or when we know that additional important support for it would probably be accessible but has not been obtained yet for one good reason or another. For this level of assurance, the essential evidence must strongly indicate that the assertion is true. We should also have no reason to expect that disconfirmation of the assertion would occur if we were to probe into the matter further.

Statements which are "more probable than not" would be accompanied by more conflicting evidence, even though we would have found good reasons for discounting the negative input and for accepting the truth of such assertions with a relatively high degree of confidence. The truth of an assertion is more probable than not when a clear majority of the evidence supports its truth. While the possibility of subsequent disaffirmance would be recognized, there should be no specific reason to expect that would happen. This level of assurance is comparable to the preponderance or greater weight of the evidence standard that is required for determinations made in civil trials in American courts.

These five levels of assurance (absolute certainty, relative certainty, effective certainty, the highly probable, and the more probable than not) comprise the main kinds of certainty which we can have in the truth of an assertion, based upon differences in their respective positive and negative criteria. When our level of confidence in the truth of a statement does not rise even to the level of "more probable than not," however, we would just be guessing about its truth (assuming that it has not been affirmatively disconfirmed).

While assigning positions along the certainty continuum to different assertions involves judgments which are to some extent subjective, this is not an arbitrary process. When we focus upon the appropriate criteria which apply to the different ranges of assurance, I believe that general agreement could be reached on the classification of the levels of assurance for many, if not most, of the assertions we believe to be true.

3. THE CERTAINTY NEEDED FOR THE CONFIRMATION OF TRUTH

Factual truth is the same for every kind of statement about every kind of fact. The different approaches that we need to take in finding and confirming truth for different kinds of statements does not impact either the final objective or the final product. They present different ways to access the single goal, which is unchanging regardless of how well or how frequently we may reach it.

Furthermore, the truth of a true statement which we have not fully confirmed is exactly the same as the truth of a true statement which we have fully confirmed. The truth about the existence of atoms ("It is true that atoms exist") has existed throughout the history of our universe (or at least as long as a consciousness would have been available to posit it), but our knowledge of that truth was only obtained through confirmations made by scientists in the early twentieth century. Prior to that time, the assertion was true; but until that time, no one could say that they had found it to be true because of the insufficiencies in the earlier confirmation efforts.

Whether we have *found* a truth requires us to consider the issue of certainty. What it takes for us to say that we know that we have found the truth for different types of statements will vary with the levels of certainty which we can attain in those confirmations. We are able to know the truth of a statement only when we reach the appropriate assurance level for it.

In my opinion, we should limit the acceptable use of statements that begin with "It is true that" only to those specific assertions which have been confirmed as best as that type of assertion can be confirmed. When we cannot draw that conclusion, we may still, in appropriate circumstances, say that the statement "might be true" or that it "seems to be true," or even that "I just believe it to be true" (which is something we often do when choices about actions are necessary); but we should not categorically say that "It is true" unless it has been confirmed to the highest degree of certainty that is available for that kind of assertion. "Truth" should simply not be ascribed to any assertion which falls short of that mark. Many such statements might be true, and we might actually be able to fully confirm the truth of some of them later; but until and unless they have been confirmed as best as that type of assertion can be confirmed, we should not represent that we have attained the truth about them but rather communicate the lesser degree of confirmation which we have reached when we are describing their factual accuracy.

While we are able to attain relative certainty or effective certainty with respect to at least some statements in most of the different types of assertions we make, we often fall short of those levels. We need to make too many determinations about truth in too little time to be able to conduct full confirmations of any significant percentage of the assertions which we must consider, so, much of the time, we will either have to be satisfied with lower levels of certainty or else live in continual frustration with our less-than-ideal truth-confirming capacities. Fortunately, as William James noted, we are often able to short-circuit the length of time involved and credit an idea with truth based upon an existing mass of verifying circumstance,[30] thereby accepting one of the levels of probability as being sufficient for our purposes at that time. Nevertheless, we can know some truths about a number of things with great assurance if we work hard enough on their confirmation. Granted, we must live with many uncertainties, and we may be disappointed in being unable to confirm or disconfirm some critically important assertions in and to our lives because of the nature of the different confirmations we can employ and because of the nature of (and inherent limits on) the mental tools we must use as we interact with the world. However, we think, as we must think, through these means; and what we can attain with their proper application is human truth. Consequently, we do not live in a world of mere belief. Rather, we live and participate in a world in which truth exists and can frequently be found.

NOTES

1. Santayana, *Realms of Being*, p. 404.
2. Popper, *Conjectures and Refutations*, p. 11. Or, as Mao Tse Tung put it, "In the great river of a man's knowledge all things are relative, and no one can grasp absolute truth." Edgar Snow, *Journey to the Beginning* (New York: Random House, 1958), p. 166.
3. True believers are highly effective in certain situations. See, e.g., Eric Hoffer, *The True Believer* (New York: Harper & Row, 1951).

4. Desmond M. Clarke, "Pascal's Philosophy of Science," *The Cambridge Companion to Pascal*, Nicholas Hammond, ed. (Cambridge University Press, 2003), p. 105. Pascal also said that "if genuine knowledge requires absolute certainty, then we know very little." Ibid.

5. Peter Alexander, "Ernst Mach," *The Encyclopedia of Philosophy*, vol. 5, p. 116.

6. See, e.g., A. J. Ayer, "Basic Propositions," *Philosophical Analysis*, 2nd ed., Max Black, ed. (Ithaca, NY: Cornell University Press, 1950), pp. 60–74.

7. Werkmeister, *The Basis and Structure of Knowledge*, p. 135.

8. Karl Popper, *The Logic of Scientific Discovery* (London: Hutchison, 1959), p. 104.

9. T. H. Huxley, *Collected Essays*, vol. VI (London: Macmillan, 1893), pp. 317–318.

10. James, "The Will to Believe," p. 47. He said that it was the only truth that Pyrrhonistic skepticism leaves standing. Ibid.

11. Russell Shorto, *Descartes' Bones* (New York: Doubleday, 2008), p. 20.

12. Bergson, "An Introduction to Metaphysics," p. 241.

13. Richard Schmitt, "Phenomenology," *The Encyclopedia of Philosophy*, vol. 6, pp. 139–140.

14. Poincare was an exception, for he wrote that "Experiment . . . alone can give us certainty." Poincare, "Science and Hypothesis," p. 238.

15. Popkin, *The History of Scepticism*, p. 101.

16. See, e.g., T. A. Goudge, "Thomas Henry Huxley," *The Encyclopedia of Philosophy*, vol. 4, p. 102; and Peter Koestenbaum, "Karl Jaspers," *The Encyclopedia of Philosophy*, vol. 4, p. 255.

17. See, e.g., Bertrand Russell, *The Problems of Philosophy* (Oxford University Press, 1964), pp. 116–17; L. J. Russell, "Gottfried Wilhelm Leibniz," *The Encyclopedia of Philosophy*, vol. 4, p. 423; and Thomas C. O'Brien, "Reginald Marie Garrigou-Lagrange," *The Encyclopedia of Philosophy*, vol. 3, p. 268.

18. Boas, *The History of Ideas*, p. 44.

19. Durant, *The Mansions of Philosophy*, pp. 26–27.

20. Bridgman, *The Way Things Are*, p. 6.

21. Werkmeister, *The Basis and Structure of Knowledge*, p. 133.

22. Dorothy Emmet, "Presuppositions of Finite Truths," Annual Philosophy Lecture, Henrietta Hertz Trust, Washington University, Read 3/16/49, p. 15.

23. John Dewey, *The Quest for Certainty* (New York: Minton, Balch & Co., 1929), p. 33.

24. Peirce, "Notes on Scientific Philosophy," p. 251.

25. The full continuum of assurance runs beyond these degrees of support for an assertion's truth through uncertainty about its truth and into degrees of probability and certainty about its falsehood; but in this chapter I am discussing certainty in truth after support for its confirmation has been obtained, so I will not be dealing with degrees of doubt about it or with degrees of certainty in the disconfirmation of a statement.

26. The "effective certainty" category will exist regardless of what we may call it. While the label could be changed to something which does not include the word "certainty," the criteria for and function of this category of assurance would not change.

27. R. M. Chisholm, "Sextus Empiricus and Modern Empiricism," *Philosophy of Science*, vol. 8, No. 3, July, 1941, p. 379.

28. James, *The Varieties of Religious Experience*, p. 332.

29. Bertrand Russell, *The Problems of Philsosphy* (London: Oxford University Press, 1964), pp. 116-17.

30. James, *The Meaning of Truth*, p. 165.

Part II

THE PROCESS OF FINDING AND CONFIRMING TRUTH

Given that we use the means described in Part I to find and confirm truths, the more adept we become in the use of those means, the more truths we should be able to confirm. In Part II, I will elaborate further on how we employ the different types of confirmation in order to determine whether any given assertion is true or false.

We constantly make mental assertions, particularly as we are confronted by events and objects to which we must respond in some way. We are also regularly presented with assertions which have been made by others (which are usually verbal but can also be nonverbal), so the need for each of us to try to find factual truth is ever-present in our lives. Sometimes, we have the luxury of an unlimited amount of time during which we can devote ourselves to the confirmation or disconfirmation of a particular assertion; but, usually, we must end these searches and decide these issues fairly quickly, either because some kind of action is required or because we need to move on to other things. The fully extended process for confirming truth that is described below can require more time and effort than we can dedicate to truth-confirming activities, but even the shortcuts which we frequently take in trying to confirm truth quickly are facilitated by an understanding of the process as a whole.

A thorough confirmation effort can be broken down into nine steps. A fully extended truth-confirmation process calls for us to:

1. *Adopt an attitude conducive to the search for truth.* When undertaking the confirmation of any specific assertion, it is important to be in a frame of mind that will assist us–and not impede us–in that effort.

2. *Frame the assertion to be considered as precisely as possible.* We need to know what a question is before we should try to answer it, so that we do not waste effort and so that we can avoid tangents and red herrings.
3. *Identify the type of assertion which is being considered.* Every assertion will fit into one or more categories of different general types of assertions, such as statements about historical events or statements about present sensations.
4. *Select the appropriate forms of confirmation.* Different kinds of confirmation are more effective in our consideration of some types of assertions than they are with others. We should determine which forms of confirmation we may need to apply with regard to a given assertion and which ones we may safely ignore.
5. *Apply the appropriate types of confirmation.* This step is, of course, the heart of the quest in the search for truth: we need to determine what happens as we consider each applicable form of confirmation for the assertion being pondered.
6. *Weigh the evidence to determine whether the assertion has been confirmed.* We frequently do not obtain uniform results from the various confirmations which we have attempted, so we need to use our best judgment in deciding whether we can consider a given assertion to have been confirmed.
7. *Determine the degree of certainty to ascribe to a confirmed assertion.* We then have to ascertain the degree of certainty which we have obtained for that assertion, because that will help us decide whether we may call it "true."
8. *Draw a conclusion about the truth of the confirmed assertion.* If the confirmation which has been achieved reaches the highest level of certainty which can be obtained for that type of statement, then we should conclude that the assertion is, indeed, true. If that level of certainty has not been attained, then we should not conclude that it is true (although we might still be able to legitimately say that we believe that it is true).
9. *Keep an open mind for new evidence that may become available in the future.* Because we sometimes err in these efforts-even when we have been as careful as possible-we should remain receptive to any new input which might affect the "truth" of assertions even after we have confirmed them.

It should be noted that this process is the same for either confirming or disconfirming the truth of a given assertion. We should be able to uncover a falsehood by using the same steps that we employ to confirm a truth. In one case, we simply formulate the assertion positively (e.g., "It is true that the tomato is red"), and, in the other case, we frame it negatively ("It is not true that the tomato is blue").

Many of these confirmation steps can be followed even when we are hurriedly trying to verify truths, particularly when we are able to speed through some of them subconsciously. The failure to follow one or more of these steps, however, may reduce our chances of successfully finding the truth of the matter and consequently lead to more overall errors in our conclusions and mistakes in our actions. Fortunately, we have developed many efficiencies in confirming assertions "on the run" (which we must often do in everyday life). A number of our routine assertions will not require any extended truth analysis, because they are the same as or quite similar to assertions which we have confirmed many times before (e.g., where the forks are located in a kitchen drawer, which streets we need to take in order to return home from work, and so forth). In most of those cases, we find it sufficient to verify new assertions almost automatically by analogy, accepting their truth through and because of their similarity to the previously confirmed statements. Another significant time-saver involves choosing to use but a single form of confirmation for an assertion, either because it is likely to be the most reliable one for that purpose or because it is the most accessible one (or both). For example, once we accept the general accuracy of a specific external authority, we often thereafter accept related assertions from that same source without seeking any independent verification of them, because we have confidence in the reliability of the source. Similarly, because we have found our physical senses to be substantially reliable, we usually do not feel the need to stop and consider whether we need to confirm the sound of the telephone ringing in any manner other than by simply hearing and recognizing that familiar ring or melody.

For those occasions when we are given pause because something feels "out of sync," however, as well as for those occasions when the outcome of a confirmation is of such importance that we want to make that decision as carefully as possible, it is useful to take each of the nine distinct steps in the fully extended truth-confirmation process.

Chapter Five

The Steps Involved in Finding and Confirming Truth

1. ADOPTING AN ATTITUDE CONDUCIVE TO THE SEARCH FOR TRUTH

We are variable in many ways, and some of those variations-especially in our feelings, moods, attitudes, and mental energy-can heavily impact our searches for truth. Therefore, truth confirmations are facilitated when we recognize those things which may hinder our efforts so that we can avoid or eliminate them, or, if we are not able to do that, either delay our conclusions until those problems would no longer affect us or factor their influence into our determinations.

An improper attitude in a search for truth can completely thwart our efforts. According to the Bacons (Roger and Francis), we should guard against dogmas, feelings, unworthy authorities, custom, popular prejudice, and narrowness of mind.[1] Of course, other attitudes and emotional factors can also be detrimental in these efforts. Positively stated, however, we should have an alert and open mind so that we will be able not only to see but also to understand input from all of the sources which are available to us for the confirmation or disconfirmation of the assertion being considered. While we may not be able to completely eliminate all potentially negative factors during a truth search, an open and self-critical attitude usually helps us obtain accurate results more consistently.

2. FRAMING THE ASSERTION TO BE CONSIDERED

When trying to confirm the truth of an assertion, it helps to have a clearly articulated version of it in front of us. While we may not need to lock ourselves

74   *Chapter Five*

into an exact or exclusive set of words, we should know the principal elements of whatever it is that we are trying to verify (or trying to disconfirm). Actually, the identification of the assertion to be considered often does not reach its final conclusion when we first find an acceptable formulation of it, because, throughout the process, as we get feedback, we may need to modify it or shift our focus. For example, an initial assertion that the cats are meowing because they are hungry and, therefore, that there must not be any food in their bowls would be disconfirmed by looking at their bowls and seeing some food in them, but we would then quickly move on to reformulate the underlying assertion being considered (dealing with why the cats were meowing) to include the possibilities that there could be something wrong with their food or that something other than food is bothering them.

Framing the assertion to be considered will sometimes be a difficult step if we are not sure exactly what it is that we are really after-or exactly what we may be able to find-until we are well into the confirmation process. Nevertheless, even in cases when we know that later adjustments may be likely, we should make the assertion which we are trying to confirm or disconfirm as clear as possible as soon as possible.

3. IDENTIFYING THE TYPE OF ASSERTION WHICH IS BEING CONSIDERED

Because we can approach the confirmation of different types of assertions in different ways, the next step is to identify the specific type of assertion that will be under review. Useful categories for this purpose include: (1) assertions which are descriptive of our present perceptions (both physical and mental ones); (2) assertions which relate to a specific point in time (that is, to the present, the past, or the future); and (3) assertions which are in some way normative. While this is not an exclusive list of the different types of factual assertions that we make,[2] many of the assertions which we are called upon to confirm every day would fall into at least one of these categories. When an assertion does so, then certain types of verification could be effectively employed in trying to confirm their truth or falsity, and others would not be.

4. SELECTING THE APPROPRIATE TYPES OF CONFIRMATION TO BE USED

Not all seven types of confirmation will be relevant for each and every kind of assertion. Intention, for example, does not provide valid or useful information for confirming or disconfirming the proposition that "It is true that George Washington was the first President of the United States of America." Because some types of confirmation are generally more effective than others with regard to certain kinds of assertions, when we are able to identify the forms of confirmation which may be useful in the consideration of an assertion, we should thereby be able to bypass the others.

Specific guidelines can be identified for each of the three categories of assertions described in the previous subsection (those about our present perceptions, those relating to events occurring at specific points in time, and those applying norms).

a. Assertions About Present Perceptions

Several forms of confirmation are almost always useful in confirming the truth of assertions about things which we can personally sense physically or apprehend mentally in some manner. First and foremost is present perception itself, because that is our immediate means of perceiving external and internal worlds. If we apprehend something through a present perception of it, we thereby find support for the truth of an assertion which alleges its existence or something about its nature or character.

Another form of confirmation which will potentially apply to most assertions about our present perceptions is reason. Induction is primarily employed in our efforts to expand our knowledge about the world by extrapolating from cumulative observations in order to reach conclusions which provide us with additional information. Through inductive inferences, we are able to generalize about groups of objects and to make predictions about individual members of those groups based upon our inductive conclusions. We also frequently use the deductive side of reason in verifying assertions about specific matters involving our present perceptions. For example, from fresh deer tracks, we can deduce that a deer recently passed along the way. Reason is especially useful in confirming assertions about present perceptions as we attempt to add more and more information and meaning to them.

External authority is the third important source of confirmation for assertions about our present perceptions. External authorities can reinforce (or undermine) both our personal perceptions and the inferences which we may make about them (for example, "That wasn't the telephone, it was the doorbell").

A fourth form of confirmation which is often employed in considering the truth or falsity of assertions about our present perceptions is memory. This is particularly true when we return in the present to a situation in which we have been before. If I remember something about the external world that I confirmed yesterday (e.g., that the tomatoes were then still green and not yet ripe) and walk outside today and take a quick look at the same plants again, my memory of the earlier truth of yesterday's perception would support the truth of today's assertion about that same thing (e.g., "It is true that the tomatoes are still green and not yet ripe").

None of the other three forms of confirmation, however, consistently provides relevant information for or against the truth of assertions about our present perceptions. While we may sometimes use one or more of them in dealing with such assertions (as someone might use intuition in trying to decide where to drill for water), the propriety or impropriety of the use of that means should become fairly obvious in each such case. Even if we intuit something about a present perception and thereby try to employ it as a confirming means, intuition will not be applicable to most of our assertions about present perceptions, because our intuitions simply do not normally provide useful information about them. The limited effectiveness of intuition on matters of present perception can be illustrated by closing your eyes in an unfamiliar space and trying to intuit your way around. Similarly, intention is of no help in confirming present perceptions. Present intentions are plainly not of any assistance in confirming most assertions about existing external objects, or else many of us would now be surrounded by pots of gold. Finally, faith, even though it may be involved in the confirmation of present perceptions in certain circumstances, does not provide supportive inferences for most such assertions.

Therefore, when dealing with statements about our own present perceptions, if we have sufficient time to do so, we should focus upon their potential confirmation or disconfirmation by means of present perception, reason, memory, and external authority. This can be done by asking questions like, "If the assertion is true, what will I perceive?"; "If it is false, what would my perceptions be?"; "Does the statement make sense, given what I already know about this kind of object?"; "Do I remember anything about it previously?"; and "Who else would be able to confirm it or disconfirm it, and how would they know?" With these inquiries, the search for the truth of assertions about our present perceptions should be able to concentrate upon the forms of confirmation which are most likely to provide successful inferences about their truth or falsity.

b. Assertions About Past, Present, and Future Events

We can also identify several guidelines which can assist us in the confirmation of assertions relating to events which occur at specific points in time. Many of our assertions do relate to such events (e.g., "I slept well last night,"

"She is in Kansas City today," "They are going to barbeque tomorrow"); but many do not (e.g., "A carpet is a floor covering made of fiber," "2 + 3 = 5"). If we determine that an assertion relates to an event which would occur at some point in time, which forms of confirmation can regularly help us decide whether that assertion is true?

If the assertion relates to something which is happening in the present, then we will usually be able to employ the same four forms of confirmation which were discussed above for statements about present sensations and perceptions: present perception, external authority, memory, and reason. "This strawberry tastes sweet" can be confirmed (or disconfirmed) by recognizing the sensation of sweetness and the perception (on a higher interpretive level) of the object being a strawberry. We can also ask others (after they take their own bites) to agree or disagree. We may remember how sweet the strawberries tasted yesterday (particularly those from the same bowl), and those recollections and the inductive support drawn from them can provide a substantiating inference for an assertion about today's event, as well. If we pick out a mushy one and refuse to eat it, then we will have used deduction ("It is true that mushy strawberries do not taste sweet; therefore, this mushy strawberry would not taste sweet"). While intention should not play a role in making a judgment about the sweetness of the strawberry, we know that our expectations can sometimes affect our assessments, and, thus, we need to be attuned to that possibility in this kind of evaluation. Intuition might also have an impact in certain situations (e.g., I may intuit that I will find someone's keys under a pillow), as might faith ("I strongly believe that they are trying to work things out"). Nevertheless, the first four forms of confirmation would likely be useful in considering almost all assertions about present conditions or events, but the last three would apply only in limited circumstances in which their relevance should become immediately apparent.

If the event in question occurred in the past, then the process of confirming or disconfirming the truth of an assertion about it consists of two steps: (1) finding support for the content of the assertion independent of its occurrence in the past (that is, as if it were a present occurrence) and (2) finding support for the recollection which is involved.

For all-past tense assertions, there was a time when the purported event either was occurring or was not occurring as a present event. To confirm or disconfirm an assertion about the past, we must determine, as best we can, what information existed at that point in the past which would tend to validate (or refute) its having occurred then. In other words, when it (whatever it was) was supposedly occurring, which forms of confirmation would then properly have been used in deciding whether the assertion about it was true? For this part of the confirmation process for past-tense assertions, we should again look primarily to present perception, reason, memory, and external authority. For example, given the assertion, "Yesterday John saw a bear," we would apply those four forms of confirmation in the same manner in which we would have used them yesterday to determine whether John was actually seeing a bear when he supposedly saw it. This first step essentially removes the assertion from its past-tense context and reviews any evidence which would have been relevant to its confirmation as a present-tense assertion.

The second step in trying to confirm assertions about the past is to determine whether the recollection process has been effective. For this step, three forms of confirmation are normally applicable. If I have an independent remembrance of an occurrence, then I use memory in this capacity. Such personal recollections may be further supported by an external authority when another person who is available for consultation has a separate remembrance or a preserved memory of the occurrence. In this context, we draw not only on the direct memories of other people but also on such things as writings or visual and audio recordings–on photographs, tapes, videos, and so forth. In addition to bolstering or undermining my confidence in my personal memories, external authorities are the only possible means of support which exists for the recollection element of the many past-tense assertions about which I have no personal memories. I do not "remember" what Jesse Owens did in the Munich Olympics in 1936 from my personal experience; but there are still some external authorities who do, and there are a number of others who reliably recorded it (such external sources do not, of course, still have to be living). Finally, we can use reason in supporting or refuting the recollection element for assertions about past occurrences. One rational test we often employ here is coherence: if a past-tense assertion coheres with other statements about the past which we have already found to be true, then, from that relationship, we infer support for the recollection process which has been involved with the new assertion. For example, if a young student hears for the first time from her history teacher that Winston Churchill met with Franklin D. Roosevelt and Joseph Stalin at Yalta in 1945 to discuss post-World War II Europe, that would probably "cohere" with what she had previously been told about those leaders; but if she were told that Churchill was a good painter, that might not initially cohere, and she would have to learn more about Churchill as a person before it would. Similarly, the truth of a past-tense assertion may be further supported if it coheres with knowledge about what is possible in the present. Any dissonance between the new assertion and accepted limitations on present possibilities would tend to disconfirm that assertion. For example, if we were told that someone had run the 100-meter dash in 9.20 seconds in 1940, we should doubt the truth of that statement, because nothing even close to that time has officially been achieved by anyone to this day.

By reviewing both of these perspectives for an assertion about the past-for the support it has independent of its tense and for the support which exists for the recollection process which has been used-we should be able to determine whether the results, in combination, are sufficient to draw an affirmative conclusion about its truth. In order to be able to consider the truth of a past-tense assertion to be confirmed, both of those elements would need significant support; but for its disconfirmation, a negative conclusion from only one of those two perspectives would be sufficient.

Finally, in this category dealing with assertions relating to events in time, we need to determine which types of confirmation can be helpful in making decisions about the truth of statements about the future, such as "It is going to rain tomorrow." The confirmation of assertions about the future, like those about the past, is also a two-step process, consisting in this case of a predictive element and of a subsequent witnessing element.

The first step, since the event has not yet occurred, is predictive, and it is somewhat analogous to the recollection element in confirmations of assertions about the past. We may use six of the forms of confirmation in considering the predictive element of a future-tense assertion. We often use present perception, memory, and reason together, the latter both inductively (e.g., "Rain often follows this type of cloud pattern") and deductively ("With the type of cloud pattern that is overhead, it's going to rain"). Coherence between a statement about the future and our present knowledge is also an important rational test for us to apply when considering its truth potential. If it appears to be possible within the limits of our current knowledge, that relationship will support its truth; but if it does not reasonably cohere, that fact would tend to disconfirm the statement. We would thus find support for "It is true that within the next 100 years, someone from Earth will land on Mars," and we would find a reason for disbelieving "It is true that within the next 100 years, someone from Earth will land on a planet near the North Star." We also frequently resort to external authorities when considering the potential truth of statements about the future, and those can include everyone from TV weathermen to racetrack tipsters. Sometimes we use reason and external authorities in combination (e.g., "Careful measurements indicate that the hole in the ozone layer has gotten progressively larger in recent years; many experts agree that a contributing cause of this phenomenon has been our use of chlorofluorocarbon chemicals; our use of those chemicals has grown this year; therefore, the ozone hole will be bigger next year"). If we can somehow affect whether that future event will or will not occur, we may also utilize intention in the confirmation of future assertions (e.g., "I'll be there in 20 minutes"). Finally, we may sometimes even use intuition if we have intuited something which deals with the future. This would include everything from the occasional sense of foreboding, which almost all of us have experienced from time to time, to an unusual facility for anticipating future events which a few people seem to possess.

The second element in confirming assertions about the future involves the support for or opposition to the truth of the assertion which can be found when the predicted event is supposed to occur. If we-or others-are around then, the assertion which was made in the past about a possible future event can then be finally confirmed or disconfirmed by employing the same types of inferences described above for present- and past-tense assertions (whichever of those would then be appropriate). If I assert "There will be a hurricane next Tuesday in Jamaica," someone who is in Jamaica next Tuesday could determine if my statement about the future had been an accurate prediction. Similarly, at a later point in time, someone could confirm or disconfirm it as a past-tense assertion by using the same tests that we employ for other assertions about past events (in this example, by reviewing available weather data that had been reported from that area for that Tuesday by external authorities). No confirmation about the truth of a future-tense assertion can be fully completed, of course, until this second "witnessing" step has been taken.

As with past-tense assertions, in order to consider the truth of a future-tense assertion to be confirmed, sufficient support would need to exist for both of the elements which are involved. In this case, that would require support for the predictive element before the future event has occurred and the subsequent confirmation of the occurrence or nonoccurrence of the predicted event at that point in the future.

By identifying the tense of assertions which deal with events which may or may not be occurring or have occurred or which will or will not occur at specific points in time, and then focusing our attention upon the forms of confirmation which are most likely to be of assistance to us in determining whether they are true, false, or simply not confirmable or disconfirmable, we are able to engage in the truth-verification process in a more efficient manner.

c. Normative Assertions

Normative assertions are those through which we ascribe qualities-like "good" or "beautiful"-to something. This broad category of statements consists of all of our value judgments, from ethics and aesthetics to politics and other practical activities (e.g., "It's true that, to hang this picture at that place on the wall, it would be best to use this special kind of hanger").

When we try to validate normative assertions, we may effectively employ five of the different types of confirmation. The most important of these is probably external authority. External authority provides almost all of our initial conceptual input for terms like "good" and "bad," "beautiful" and "ugly"-indeed, for all of our values. To a large extent, we learn the meanings and functions of normative concepts through social interaction, and society continues to arbitrate these matters throughout our lifetimes (as well as long before and long after them). External authorities can also support or undermine the truth of many of our specific assertions when we apply those values.

Both intuition and faith may also be used. General normative rules and their applications may both be intuited, in which event intuition can provide a separate basis and means for confirmation of such an assertion (e.g., "It just didn't feel right for me to put our money into that proposed deal"). When we use faith in efforts to confirm normative assertions, our strong beliefs in general precepts or in their applications can be supportive of the confirmation of those assertions (e.g., "I strongly believe that it would be bad to do that kind of thing!").

Memory will be involved in all of these value assertions, as we recall and compare general values which we have accepted regarding that normative area or remember other specific judgments that we have previously made about similar things.

Many people have tried to find rational bases for our values, seeking to justify them by some logical criterion. Rational support can be cited, for example, for both the golden rule and the golden mean. Reason's role in the confirmation of truth in this area may, however, be more important in the application of our norms to our everyday lives. We deduce from general premises whether a particular choice or action is, for example, "good." For instance, from "It is good to share," I may deduce, while eating from a box of cookies, that it would be good to share some of them with the person who is sitting next to me.

Some people object to the application of the word "truth" to normative assertions. While those taking this position allege a lack of meaning in the use of the word in conjunction with these statements, their concern may relate more to the lesser degrees of certainty which we usually are able to obtain for the truth of normative statements. But less certainty about their confirmation-or less verifiability-does not mean total unverifiability. We use, and we continue to find meaning in using, "truth" in its factual sense in connection with many of our statements about values. (We certainly argue often enough over whether particular normative assertions are "true," as when we debate whether cutting taxes or raising taxes would be a good thing.)

When we assert the truth or falsity of normative statements, we improve our chances of confirming or disconfirming their truth or falsity by applying the five forms of confirmation set out above. Neither present perception nor intention would provide relevant information for these purposes, however.

When an assertion falls into more than one of these three categories (a normative assertion about a painting we are presently viewing, for example), the potential usefulness of the forms of confirmation would be cumulative. Consequently, when considering a normative assertion about a material object (e.g., "It is true that this is a painting which is beautiful"), we should pursue its confirmation through present perception, external authority, memory, reason, intuition, and faith, the first four due to their potential applicability not only to assertions about present perceptions and present-tense statements but also to normative assertions, and the last two because of their potential applicability to normative assertions.

These guidelines do not present hard-and-fast rules but rather provide general directions for this part of the confirmation process. The search for truth which involves one or more of these three major categories of assertions can be facilitated by the early identification of the types of confirmation which may be productively used in each such case. If we determine that an assertion concerns a present perception or that it relates to an event in time or has normative content, then we should apply the specific means which are most likely to help us in our efforts to confirm or disconfirm it.

5. APPLYING THE APPROPRIATE TYPES OF CONFIRMATION

After having determined which forms of confirmation may be most relevant to the assertion under consideration, the next step is to apply them. The actual application of appropriate forms of confirmation to specific assertions is neither an exact science nor a precise craft, however. Some of the potential problems which we face as we undertake this phase of the truth-confirmation process were discussed in Chapter 3 in the context of questions about the validity of each of the different approaches in the confirmation of truth. For example, when using intuition as support for the truth of a statement, we need to try to be sure that we intuited it rather than obtained it in some other manner. Fortunately, by taking some of the specific precautions discussed below, we should be able to avoid or minimize many of the errors which could result from the inherent weaknesses in each of the major forms of truth confirmation. This section also includes suggestions on ways in which we may enhance the effectiveness of our use of each of these means.

a. Present Perception

We can reduce the number and impact of mistakes that we make in our assertions about present perceptions of the external world and of our mental states by taking the following steps when using this first means of truth confirmation:

(1) *Try to repeat the perception.* When a "retake" produces the same results as the original perception, it provides additional support for the truth of the assertion about that perception. This support derives not only from the cumulative effect of a second, similar perception, but also from the fact that we more strongly focus our attention on the object of that perception during any repeated attempt to perceive it. We are thereby more likely to disregard the competing stimuli which may have affected our original impressions.

(2) *Try to rule out the potential presence of some of the principal sources of perceptual mistakes.* If we are dreaming, having an illusion, or suffering from an hallucination or if we have been hypnotized, then what we believe to be a present perception may be in error. Fortunately, we are normally able to recognize dreams, illusions, hallucinations, and hypnotic states after we may have had them by appealing to reason, memory, and external authority in conjunction with any new present perceptions we may have about an external object or an internal mental state. Consequently, in "real life," we can always stop and look for indications that one of those things may be occurring. If we do discover something which we know may have led to an erroneous perception, we may thereby be able to disconfirm the assertion. If we do not discover any of them, then we will have reduced-if not totally eliminated-their possibility; and that information provides additional support for the confirmation of the truth of the assertion about that perception.

The same approach applies to problems associated with confusion, fatigue, and other physical and/or mental conditions or impairments which can sometimes affect our perceptions about present sensations or mental states. We can usually recognize when, for example, we are fatigued; and if we find that we are, we may be able to defer making any conclusions about an assertion dealing with that perception until we are more rested (if that is possible), or else try to summon up some of our energy reserves to overcome the fatigue so that we will have a better chance of analyzing things correctly. While we have to make our own peace with evil-demon and brain-in-a-vat arguments ahead of time, we should be able to effectively address the other sources of errors which we may make about present perceptions as part of the confirmation process.

(3) *Try to consult an external authority about it.* Assertions about present perceptions may be supported or undermined by information which competent external authorities might be able to provide to us. We believe that we have obtained support for the truth of an assertion about something we are seeing, for example, if we ask other persons who are in a position to observe the same object whether they see it, too, and they respond that they do-particularly if

they report something about its characteristics which we have not mentioned but have also perceived. Similar assistance may also be available for assertions about present mental states, as when someone else is able to help us sort out any confused feelings we may be having. Conversely, we would tend to disconfirm an assertion about a present perception if the external authority reports a conflicting perception about it or if the external authority provides a good reason for us to believe that we may be misapprehending the situation in some way-especially if we considered the truth of that assertion to have been somewhat questionable in the first place.

(4) *Review the inferences being made about the meaning of the perception.* Raw sensations must be interpreted in order to be meaningful. The shiny, brightly colored round object with a hook at the top becomes a Christmas tree ornament through the context that we provide to those perceptions. By making these inferences more explicit (as in "This is a colorful ball with a hook on top; a Christmas tree ornament is a colorful object which is often round and which is placed on the tree by means of a hook or a string; therefore, this is a Christmas tree ornament"), we can review them for possible errors either in the acceptability of their premises or in the application of the logic. If we discover that a key element is missing from a minor premise (e.g., there is no hook or string on the round object), then we will have found a reason for either disconfirming or holding in abeyance our conclusion about the proposed interpretive aspects of the assertion. On the other hand, expressly finding the premises to be valid and the logic to have been correctly applied should help confirm the truth of that assertion.

While not all of these precautions are available to us for every perception of a sensation or of a mental state (e.g., the object may have moved out of sight, or no external authority may have noticed it), by taking them when we can do so, we are often able to find additional information which is useful in our attempts to confirm assertions about our present perceptions.

b. Memory

Confirmation of an assertion by means of memory depends upon being able to recall something which substantiates a present assertion made about an event that is believed to have occurred (or not occurred) in the past.

While we will not be able to remember everything, each of us can increase the number of memories which will later be available to us by focusing hard on a present thought-to inscribe it more deeply into our memories-and thereafter by bringing it up with some repetitive regularity in order to keep it there. We can also increase the effectiveness of our recall of memories by employing various mnemonic tools–for example, by giving memories specific tags which help us find our way back to them later. Another memory-assisting technique involves alternating strenuous concentration (as we focus hard on trying to find a memory that we know should be in there somewhere) with a forced abandonment of the effort (so that we can wait for a spontaneous recall to happen, if and whenever it will).

When we have a specific memory which relates to the assertion in question, our confirmation of it may be assisted by taking three additional precautions:

(1) *Test the recollection against related memories.* Memories are interrelated, so we may find support for or refutation of the truth of an assertion about the past to the extent that a given memory coheres or fails to cohere with other memories from around the same time. If I am trying to remember enough to confirm the assertion, "It is true that I took care of my dog when I was a young child," it helps to remember the place where she was fed, which, in turn, may trigger memories of how often I see my parents rather than me delivering her food and water, in which event I would be forced to modify the assertion under consideration to "It is true that I sometimes took care of my dog" in order to make it positively confirmable.

(2) *Test the memory against what is possible in the present.* This is another coherence test of memory. By reviewing assertions about a past event in this way, we may be able to disconfirm the memory if what it purports to recall is presently impossible or to discredit it if it is highly improbable. If I "remember" shoveling the snow off my driveway in only one hour last year, but this year it takes me two hours, and if the driveway, the amount and kind of snow, and I have not changed much over that period of time, then I would have a good reason to consider the alleged truth of my assertion about that memory to have been refuted.

(3) *Refer to external authorities.* External authorities can assist us with confirmation by memory in three ways. In the first place, if such an authority independently presents either a similar or a conflicting memory, we find support or impairment, respectively, for our primary assertion. In this context, we should remember that external authorities are not only other people but also the things that we or they may have made which preserve memories, such as writings, photographs, recordings, and so forth. Secondly, an external authority may be able to provide us with some associated memories which we may not have recalled independently but which now may constitute additional reasons for accepting the truth or falsity of the assertion due to its coherence or lack of coherence with them. Finally, some of the input from external authorities may in turn stimulate our independent recall (or a "new remembrance") of a memory ("Oh, that's right! *Now* I remember what happened!").

The mental faculty of memory is required for intelligent thought, including all communication. It is always, however, suspect as a method of truth confirmation to some degree, because we know that our memories can fail and that they sometimes play tricks on us. Nevertheless, memory is indispensable to our search for truth, and its effectiveness as a form of truth confirmation may be enhanced by following the precautions discussed above.

c. Reason

Rational verification may be better employed when we take certain steps to enhance the likelihood of making correct deductions and inductions.

(1) Deductions

[a] *Identify and evaluate the premises.* With any deduction, it is important to identify the specific premises which are involved and to consider the support that exists for our acceptance of them. A properly concluded deduction is only as good as its premises, so we should begin by determining how well the premises have been stated and to what extent they have been validated. While the syllogism, "All men have two heads; John is a man; therefore, John has two heads" is logically correct, it does not help us in the search for truth because of the error in the major premise.

[b] *Review the logic.* We should also look for the common types of logical problems and errors which may occur so that we may eliminate them and thereby become more confident that the conclusion is correct-unless, of course, we find that such a problem exists. Errors in deductive reasoning would include such things as affirming the consequent ("If A, then B; B, therefore A") or denying the consequent ("If A, then B; not A, therefore not B").

Sometimes logical errors are not readily apparent because formal logic can be quite complicated, but many logical errors are relatively easy to spot if we try. If our syllogism is, "All dogs make a barking noise; I hear a barking noise; therefore, a dog is making it," then our error has been one of basic logic (since we might, for example, be hearing a parrot or a person imitating a dog); and we should catch as many of those as we can.

[c] *Take extra precautions when using coherence for the validation of an assertion.* The coherence theory of truth provides a valuable deductive tool in testing for it. However, when we use coherence in this manner, we need to try to identify the other assertions or groups of assertions (which can be called the "base assertions") to which the one in question will or will not cohere. Finding all (or even most) of these base assertions is not easy and may be impossible, and even trying to do that can be quite time-consuming (e.g., trying to restate all the physics we need to know before learning about quarks). Fre-

quently with coherence, we are able to rely either on an almost intuitive sense that a new assertion does or does not fit in or on our belief that the assertion under consideration must fit in if it does not fairly quickly become apparent to us that it does not fit in. Even if we are relying on either of these short-cut inferences, however, it can still help if we try to expressly identify and consider the related statements in the context of the purported fit. If we successfully identify significant base assertions, we can directly review whether the new assertion under consideration really coheres with them. When involved with coherence tests, however, we also need to understand why the base assertions have been accepted as being true (that is, the status of their own confirmations), so that we can have a reason for believing-if the coherence has been successful-that we have obtained something more than mere consistency. In addition, because most of the knowledge against which we will test a new assertion's coherence will have come to us through external authorities, those origins will need to be factored into the evaluation, as well.

[d] *Take extra precautions when using a pragmatic test.* The pragmatic test for truth may provide verification for a statement by determining whether it "works" or "satisfies." This approach is particularly useful when we intentionally try to affect other people or things. "It is true that my saying a kind word to Barbara makes her feel better" is supported by seeing Barbara seem to feel better when I thank her for her good efforts. "It is true that using a two-inch nail holds two boards of this size together" is confirmed, to a substantial extent, if I nail the two boards together with a two-inch nail, and they hold. When we use a pragmatic test, however, we need to make sure that what we have proposed might really affect (or has really affected) the other person or thing in a causal manner and not merely have been coincidental in time (e.g., "It is true that, if I close my eyes tonight, the sun will rise tomorrow").

The perennial problem of pragmatism is understanding and recognizing what it is that "works" or is "successful," and this problem also plays a role in any current confirmation efforts along these lines. In order to be able to recognize when something has passed a pragmatic test, we have to determine exactly what it is that satisfactorily "works" or would be "successful" for that assertion. If we cannot articulate what that accomplishment would entail and how we could recognize it, then we probably will not be able to make much use of any pragmatic test for that assertion.

[e] *Take extra precautions when using a "clear and distinct" test.* If we use the rationalists' clarity and distinctness criterion for truth ("Assertions that are as clear and distinct as Assertion J are true; Assertion M is as clear and distinct to me as is Assertion J; therefore, Assertion M is true"), we should also, at the very least, do our best to confirm or disconfirm the assertion or assertions being used as the standard (here, Assertion J). If there are problems with

the assertion or assertions that are being used for purposes of the comparison, then the support for the truth of the new assertion is eroded accordingly, and some other touchstone should be sought. In addition, we should be sure that we are identifying the existence of "clarity" and "distinctness" properly and not, for example, engaging in wishful thinking or letting an emotional desire for the assertion to be true color our analysis.

(2) Inductions

[a] *Review the factual data.* To improve our success with confirmations using inductive logic, we should examine the support which exists for assertions about the individual facts being considered. When trying to gather enough data for an initial hypothesis, we need to be careful as we make our observations and measurements. If we want to know how many pick-up trucks there are in town, we need to be sure that we look at a number of vehicles that are in the town and correctly identify those that are pick-up trucks. When it is very important to be right, or when we have some doubt about the data, we may want to repeat the tests or gather new samples.

[b] *Review the logic.* Once satisfied that we may have confidence in the underlying fact-finding process, we should then ask whether the proposed inductive conclusion can be confirmed by the particular facts which are available to us. Another question would be whether the sampling size has been sufficient. For example, have we looked at enough vehicles in enough parts of town to make a good conclusion about how many pick-up trucks there are in the entire town if we are trying to use induction to reach that conclusion rather than counting them all? In order to heed this precaution, we may also need to learn-or refresh ourselves on-some of the basic principles of statistics.

[c] *Try to disconfirm any tentative inductive conclusion.* Another step involves looking for any evidence which might disprove a tentative inductive conclusion, especially when we have one that does not quite feel right. If, up until now, all the tulips we have ever seen have been red and we have therefore preliminarily concluded that "All tulips are red," we would need to expand our search area in order to gather available information about tulips located elsewhere which might be of different colors.

[d] *Take extra precautionary steps when using the scientific method.* The scientific method includes several additional safeguards aimed at assuring the validity of inductive conclusions. In addition to the above suggestions, when employing the scientific method, we should also: (a) ask what alternative hypotheses may exist to explain the facts; (b) justify the selection of the hypothesis which is to be tested; and (c) test any other potentially valid

alternative hypothesis. The scientific method requires rigorous preparation of its inductive testing procedures; it insists upon precision, and it always asks the relevancy of the specific test being used. Finally, we should recall that no results of the scientific method should be accepted unless the tests are replicable and that it is far better, for confirmation purposes, if they are not only replicable but also have been independently replicated.

Rational verifications require special care and attention because the degree of their inferential assistance will vary directly with the skill with which we have employed them. Logic is the most objective type of interpersonal confirmation that is available to us because its applications are more demonstrably correct or incorrect than are those provided by the other forms of confirmation. We are better able to distinguish between the correctness or incorrectness of supposedly rational inferences if we are both precise and careful in our uses of deduction and induction.

d. Intuition

Intuition's inferential value is derived from its status as a trusted source of truth. If an assertion comes to us intuitively, then we may, if we have personally found our intuitions to be true more often than not (particularly with regard to that kind of subject matter), infer that the possibility of its truth has been supported.

The key to the effective use of confirmation by intuition is to determine whether an assertion was really produced intuitively. Intuitive assertions are recognizable by their spontaneity and strength, accompanied by the absence of any indication that they may have been produced by some other mental faculty or resource. In order to minimize error in applying this form of confirmation, we should try to eliminate all other possible sources of the thought (particularly those of memory and external authority). If, upon close examination, we are able to discount the other sources, then we should be able to attribute the same level of support for the truth of that statement that we give to our other accepted intuitions.

e. External Authority

External authorities do not always rise to the level of those whom we consider to be "experts." Rather, they may simply be other people who happen to be in a good position to know something or to help us prove or disprove something. Everyone can be useful in this regard, depending upon what it is that we are trying to confirm.

Special precautions to take when trying to confirm an assertion through an external authority include the following:

(1) *Test the authority for accuracy.* We first have to try to discern the degree to which the other person has accurately confirmed the assertion which he or she is making. We all know that, from time to time, everyone says things which may be–and which, from time to time, are-inaccurate to some degree. We also know that some people say "'A is B' is true" when they have little or no basis for doing so through any personal confirmation efforts they have made, and we know that some will say that "'A is B' is true" simply because they want it to be true. Therefore, we need to try to ascertain whether the person making the assertion knows that "A is B" is true or whether he or she merely believes or hopes that "A is B" is true.

Each specific external authority who might be available should, therefore, be measured for accuracy and adequacy as a source of true assertions. This should be done both initially, when someone is first being considered as a source of true assertions, and subsequently, to determine whether that person's level of success is being maintained. If a weather forecaster has had a good record of predictions over the last two weeks, she will be believed by many of her viewers; but, following several missed predictions six months later, it might behoove them to critically review her accuracy again.

(2) *Compare the credibility levels of various authorities.* When we are able to consult more than one external authority for the confirmation of a particular assertion or a particular type of assertion, we should compare their levels of accuracy and select those who are able to provide the most reliable information regarding the specific kind of assertion under consideration. For example, if we need an eyewitness to testify about an automobile accident, it would be best to use one who has both good vision and a good memory.

(3) *Consult several different authorities, particularly on the bigger questions.* It often helps to get input from multiple sources (if they are available) for our most important truth-confirmation efforts. When the positions of several reliable external authorities converge, our confidence in their conclusions about the truth of the statement under consideration is enhanced, while, when they diverge, it is diminished (unless the divergence is otherwise explicable).

(4) *Double-check the advice of external authorities for bias.* Whenever any important assertion is supported by an external authority, we may need to conduct a special review in order to assure ourselves that neither the self-interest of that authority nor any other influence or bias could be inordinately affecting its position. Most external authorities have their own objectives for most of their actions-including advice giving; so it would be difficult to find one without any self-interest or bias at all. The key is to be alert to indications that the adviser's self-interests or biases are controlling the advice. One

precaution would be to check with someone else who is known to have, or who is likely to have, a different opinion on the subject in order to uncover potentially valid criticisms of or inconsistencies in the opinion of the authority being considered. Even though an excellent baseball scout may have rated a pitching prospect highly, if that pitcher happens to be related to the scout, a general manager would clearly need to obtain the opinion of one or more unrelated scouts or pitching coaches on the young man's prospects before offering him a contract with a large signing bonus.

(5) *Watch for signs of doubts and lies.* We know that people sometimes want to deceive us or otherwise mislead us. Therefore, when we are trying to understand what someone else means when they tell us that "It is true that 'X is Y,'" we need to consider whether they are honestly making that statement, whether they may be lying about it, or whether they may be shading the truth in some way. We should, therefore, be sensitive to clues and evidence about doubting and lying in others when we turn to them as external authorities. Changes in the tone of voice or in body language (e.g., averting one's eyes or showing unusual nervousness) sometimes help us determine when a lie is being told long before we may come across other reasons for disbelieving the assertion being made by that authority.

External authorities provide one of the most useful sources of truth and one of the best means for the confirmation of truth, as well. They may also be the most dangerous means of confirmation, however, given the nature of the world in which we live. Nevertheless, if we take the above precautions when we are consulting external authorities for purposes of the confirmation of specific assertions, we should increase the likelihood of our success in making them.

f. Faith

Faith obtains its only role in the confirmation of truth through the special support that it provides for the existence of truth in strongly held beliefs. When considering whether the truth of a particular assertion may be supported on the basis of faith, we need to determine whether our belief in the truth of the assertion is really a matter of faith. To do this, we must ascertain the success or failure of other forms of confirmation with regard to the assertion, because faith plays its most important role when assertions are not fully validated some other way.

More importantly, we also have to try to determine whether a strongly held belief may be disconfirmed or shaken by reference to other forms of confirmation. If either disconfirmed or shaken, the result would no longer be a strongly held belief; and, therefore, the assertion could then no longer be confirmed by faith. Correspondingly, however, if a rigorous disconfirmation effort fails, our confidence in the validity of that assertion through a confirming inference of faith should grow.

g. Intention

If, and only if, we are dealing with the specific type of assertions to which intention may properly be applied as confirmation (that is, those dealing with present or future situations which we might purposefully affect) can we consider intention as a source of confirmation. Thus, the first safeguard in using intention in this manner is to determine whether we really have a chance of affecting the outcome. This potential may sometimes be identified by accompanying phrases like "If you only try" or "If we try hard enough."

As an additional precaution, we should also answer the following question: Are we hoping for something that we *really* want, or, in other words, would the consequences be highly agreeable or satisfying to us in one way or another? If not, the impact of intention as confirmation may be diminished, because we would be less likely to make the kind of effort which would be necessary to cause the intended outcome to come to pass (although this factor would vary with the degree of effort that would be involved).

In summary, when we use each of the seven kinds of confirmation, we can guard against inferential mistakes by carefully considering the particular problems and weaknesses that are inherent in each of them. If we do not dispose of potential errors during this part of the confirmation process, the consequences of our less-than-rigorously made decisions may appear later at what might then become inopportune moments of choice or action.

6. WEIGHING THE EVIDENCE TO DETERMINE WHETHER THE ASSERTION HAS BEEN CONFIRMED

After identifying and applying the relevant forms of confirmation to the assertion in question, the next step is to sort through the results and see if we are able to make a preliminary decision about its truth or falsity. We sometimes find ourselves confronted with conflicting results from the inferences we have made as we have tried to confirm an assertion. Whether this happens because different conclusions are supported by different types of confirmation or because different tests or sources produce different results within a single type of confirmation, we then have the task of trying to determine whether, based upon the conflicting evidence, we may still be able to conclude that the assertion appears to be true or that it appears to be false, or whether we should conclude that we do not now know enough to draw either of those conclusions.

The process of weighing the evidence can be facilitated initially by dividing the relevant inferences into three categories: those which support the truth of the assertion, those which would disconfirm it, and those which are inconclusive. If, in every confirmation effort, the results fell into only one of these three categories, our truth-finding jobs would be relatively easy. Many do not, however, so we then need to decide whether a determination about the truth of that assertion is possible at all. Sometimes not much deliberation is necessary to reach a conclusion because of the clear direction of the inferences. However, when we are faced with a number of different inferential results (e.g., inferences A and B support the truth of the assertion, but inferences C and D do not cut either way, and inference E tends to refute it), we should then consider the relative force behind each of them. We can place varied weights on the relevant inferences in a number of ways. We may value one inference more highly than others due to the type of confirmation which is involved, for example, because some forms of confirmation are generally more reliable and useful than others–particularly with regard to certain types of assertions, as discussed above. For instance, if we are dealing with medical assertions, we are likely to ascribe a higher weight to those supported by confirmations made through scientific inductions than to those supported only by intuition (unless, perhaps, the scientific result is highly negative). We may formally structure this weighing process by applying relative values to the underlying forms of the inferences, or we may more informally handle it by simply being sensitive to the fact that the degree of reliance to be placed on an inference derived from one type of confirmation need not be the same as the degree of reliance to be placed upon an inference drawn in another manner. The different weights may also be based upon how reliable certain sources or methods have proven to be in the past. This is especially true of external authorities: we frequently come to rely on some experts more than on others, and we, therefore, give more weight to the information which we receive from those whom we have learned to trust than we do to information from those whom we do not trust as much (even though they may both be experts with regard to that particular type of assertion).

I would be remiss in leaving the subject of weighing the evidence without expressly recognizing the fact that even the most careful and meticulous truth confirmations will not always produce clear answers. We live in a world of many uncertainties, and sometimes the only proper conclusion we can draw about whether an assertion is true or false is that we simply do not know. At that point, we have three choices: (1) we can draw a conclusion anyway, which we often do when a choice is required by a certain point in time by external conditions or events, like a reporting deadline, in which event we usually choose the alternative that has been supported by the greater weight of the evidence, even though it may fall short of the degree of confirmation which would be needed for a solid truth conclusion; (2) we can defer a final decision as long as possible and keep looking for other supporting or disconfirming inferences; or (3) we can modify the assertion so that the inferential conclusions which we do have will either support or disconfirm the new one. An example of the last alternative would be, upon determining that we did not have enough support for either confirming or denying the assertion that "The defendant intentionally hurt the plaintiff," we might find that we are still able to conclude whether "The defendant carelessly hurt the plaintiff" is true or false.

Weighing conflicting inferential results may not be a science, but it is a skill, and it is one that improves with experience. We advance our capabilities for drawing conclusions about factual truths by conducting reviews of the truth inferences which are available to us and then making decisions about them carefully and critically. Fortunately, as we mature, we become more adept in making these judgments-particularly in weighing conflicting evidence. And we usually make truth determinations accurately, even when we make them quickly or semi-automatically (e.g., most of us land in chairs when we sit down).

7. DETERMINING THE DEGREE OF CERTAINTY TO ASCRIBE TO A CONFIRMED ASSERTION

When we have concluded that an assertion has been confirmed, we should assess how certain we are about that result. Different levels exist in the confidence we may have in the correctness of our decisions, and they extend across a range of assurance that we can find, from relative certainty in a statement's truth to a mere probability that it is true. By assessing the inferential support for the truth of the statement using the applicable criteria for the different kinds of confirmation conclusions we may draw, as discussed in Chapter 4, we are able to conclude whether our efforts have reached relative certainty, effective certainty, or one of the two probability levels with regard to that assertion.

Because ascribing the correct level of certainty to a confirmed assertion is critical to any conclusion about its truth, this step should be carefully completed. While determining which degree we should ascribe to a specific assertion that we believe we have confirmed, we should also identify the highest degree of certainty which is attainable for that type of assertion. For example, if an assertion involves a present sensation, then if the confirmation effort has reached the level of effective certainty, it would have been fully confirmed; but if it has not reached effective certainty, then it will not have been fully confirmed.

8. DRAWING A CONCLUSION ABOUT THE TRUTH OF THE ASSERTION

A final decision on whether we have found the truth or falsity of any given assertion is not possible until we have not only determined whether an assertion has been confirmed (Step 6) but also have ascribed the appropriate degree of certainty to the conclusion which we have drawn (Step 7). It is only when we have made both of those determinations that we can ascertain whether the confirmation of the assertion under consideration has reached the highest level of assurance that we can obtain for that type of assertion. If that is the case, then, and only then, should we conclude that the assertion is indeed true. If the confirmation has not reached that level, however, then we should modify or qualify our conclusion about its truth appropriately (e.g., "I believe that 'A is B' is true for very good reasons, but I cannot yet conclusively call it true"). Once again, this conclusion is about whether we have actually found the truth of a matter and not whether a truth about it exists, because the latter is independent of the successes or failures of our confirmation efforts. But this conclusion is critical to making any declaration about whether we have indeed found the truth of the matter ourselves.

9. KEEPING AN OPEN MIND FOR FUTURE EVIDENCE THAT MAY LATER HAVE AN IMPACT ON THAT TRUTH CONCLUSION

We know that we sometimes err when we conclude that certain statements are true or false. Because of this recognized fallibility, we need to remain receptive to the later discovery of facts which could affect the inferences upon which we have relied. While we should not often have to do this for assertions which have been confirmed to the degree of relative certainty, as the certainty levels diminish, this step may become more and more important. When we find out, for example, that someone upon whose input we had relied has been lying to us, we must go back and ascertain whether that fact undermines our truth conclusion.

This last part of the confirmation process is a continual one, and it should not end as long as we value truth. If we come across important new information about a statement that we have previously accepted as being true, we may need to repeat the applicable step or steps of this truth-confirmation process again (although we can often then do that in a highly accelerated fashion).

We usually complete the process of confirming or disconfirming the truth of a given assertion fairly quickly. When I burn my hand on the stove, I do not need much reflection to know whether the assertions that "I just burned my hand on the stove" and "My hand hurts" are true. Because the world presents us with many situations in which our assertions are less clearly true or false, however, it is beneficial to know more about the process of truth confirmation and how we may best employ it.

While the truth-confirmation process in particularly difficult areas often requires a group effort (in rocket science, for example), we nevertheless always need to be able to effectively find and confirm truth by ourselves. Not only will there be occasions when others cannot help us much, but we are also often confronted with conflicting accounts about what they believe the truth to be. Even well-intentioned people without ulterior motives will sometimes disagree about factual truth: one will say, "It is true that the music is loud," and another will say, "No, it's not"; some will say, "It is true that secondary smoke from cigarettes causes a lot of lung cancer," and others will say, "No, it isn't." While we may not always have a perfect way in which to ascertain some factual truths by ourselves, we should be able to understand and use the different inferential means which are available to each of us in confirming or disconfirming the truth of every assertion by ourselves, as best we can. As with most skills, the more we try to do this, the better we should become at doing it. As we exercise our capacities for finding truth with an understanding of the full process which may be employed in order to reach it, so we should also be able to watch our individual abilities to confirm truths grow.

NOTES

1. Roger Bacon, *Compendium of the Study of Philosophy*, Thomas S. Maloney, ed. (New York: E. J. Brill,1988), p. 39; Arthur Johnson, ed., *Francis Bacon* (New York: Schocken Books, 1965), pp. 84–89.

2. Others include, but would not be limited to, a priori, hypothetical, and conditional statements.

Part III

SO, WHAT IS TRUTH?

Having reviewed how we confirm the truth of factual assertions, it is now time to revisit the most fundamental theoretical question of truth itself: "What is 'truth'?"

Thinking produces thoughts, which are mental formulations and representations. When a consciousness has a mental representation of something and also has a desire to put that mental representation to use (for example, when the conscious being is hungry and perceives something which could serve as food), it will want that mental representation to be accurate, because, if it is accurate, then that conscious being will be more likely to obtain its desired objective. The benefits of achieving a high degree of correlation between the thought and the thing thought about become apparent to every thinking being who wants anything at all. Only a completely indifferent thinking being would have no use for accuracy in its mental representations; but few such beings could even be imagined, and we humans are certainly not among them.

It, therefore, follows that if a conscious being is capable of ideation, then it will-at least at times-want and need to know whether a given assertion is accurate. This is a basic consequence of all thinking in its functional context. Accurate thinking is successful thinking. If we could not know when our assertions are true, then we simply would not be able to function very well or very long in the world.

Truth is, therefore, not only something that exists when we think it: rather, it also exists because we think. Truth seeking is one of the primary activities of every consciousness. Truth is universally coextensive with intelligent life, and it exists in and for all human beings regardless of differences in language, semantics, culture, or any other possible variables. It is an inherent and necessary consequence of the thinking process, and thus of consciousness.

When a consciousness is capable of abstract thought-of thinking about concepts-that consciousness can go beyond the basic functional use of truth and attempt to comprehend meaningful ideas on another level. This includes, among other things, the concept of factual truth itself and ideas about how to distinguish between truth and falsity. Because having a better understanding of the concept of truth should facilitate the ability to find and confirm it, the study of truth is a natural and necessary function of developed intelligence.

Chapter Six

The Basic Definition of "Truth"

While certain dictionary definitions of factual truth were employed in the previous chapters for the purpose of examining the means available to us for the confirmation of truth, I now want to consider further what, in fact, "truth" is. Precise definitions are not only important for us intellectually but also because they facilitate our use of those concepts. The better our understanding of the concept of truth, the better we are able to see our objective; and the better we see our objective, the more often we should be able to attain it. Therefore, it is important at this point to ascertain whether the word "truth" may be any more precisely defined.

If my description of the confirmation process has been correct and if it is also of general applicability (which it should be, if it is correct), then it would be appropriate to utilize that same process here, as well. In this chapter, I, therefore, intend to follow same confirmation steps which were described in Chapter 5 as I try to identify and confirm the basic definition of "truth."

STEP 1. ADOPT AN ATTITUDE CONDUCIVE TO THE SEARCH FOR TRUTH.

When a serious effort to understand something is being made, we have started the process on the right foot. Anytime we take the time to write about the meaning of something, we are giving it a good deal of serious attention, as is appropriate.

Another issue in this first step is to consider potential feelings and attitudes which could adversely influence our search. Few of us can completely eliminate all of the possible impediments to an honest and thorough effort to confirm an assertion, given our predilection to like or dislike things and our inclinations to try to pick winners and avoid losers quickly. But a self-critical review of these things can move us in the proper directions, although it may sometimes take input from others to get us back on track, particularly if we tend to succumb to "unworthy authorities" or "popular prejudices."

I believe that I began with, and that I have tried to maintain throughout this process, an attitude which is conducive to making this a successful effort, or one which at least does not bring a high risk of scuttling it, although I need to be alert for bias which may have developed due to the amount of time and effort that I have already put into this project.

STEP 2. FRAME THE ASSERTION UNDER CONSIDERATION AS PRECISELY AS POSSIBLE.

At the beginning of this book, I accepted as a working definition of factual truth that it is "conformity with fact," "agreement with reality," "the real state of affairs," and "accuracy of delineation or representation." For the purpose of framing the assertion to be considered in this particular confirmation effort, I will use the standard historical approach to the concept's definition: that truth is essentially the quality or characteristic of an assertion which is present when that which the statement asserts conforms with the facts about that thing. This is, of course, but one way in which to state what is called the "correspondence theory" of truth. The essence of that theory can be formulated in many different ways, including "An assertion is true if the statement of fact that it proposes agrees with that fact." "Truth" would then be what we have found when a given statement meets that test. However, because the essence of this concept can be characterized in a number of different ways, the actual assertion which I will be testing in this chapter will be the following one: "It is true that the cluster of assertions which variously state the correspondence theory of truth do accurately indicate what truth–in its factual context-really is."

STEP 3. IDENTIFY THE TYPE OF ASSERTION BEING CONSIDERED.

The statement that is set out in step 2 does not fit into any of the three general categories of assertions which I described in Chapter 5, because it does not deal with a present perception, it does not relate to events occurring at a specific point in time, and it is not a normative statement (as that is typically defined). Rather, it is a statement about the meaning of a word which represents a concept.

STEP 4. SELECT THE APPROPRIATE TYPES OF CONFIRMATION TO BE USED.

Because the statement at issue does not fall within any of the three categories identified above, I am unable to utilize the short cuts which I described for determining the forms of confirmation to be applied to it. Consequently, for this one, I will need to consider all of them.

Here, we are trying to establish whether an assertion about the definition of a word is true. The word in question represents (according to the correspondence statements) a concept reflecting our understanding of a relationship which exists between a conscious representation about something and that something itself. The examination must, therefore, focus upon our language. Because words are social instruments which are established and maintained by social convention, we will need to consult and consider external authorities on these matters. In addition, however, we should try to find effective input from reason (e.g., we can consider how this concept fits in with other related concepts that we have) and intuition (for we also may have some intuitive insight into a concept).

The other four forms of confirmation do not appear to me to be likely to offer any effective assistance in this effort. Because a concept is neither a personal mental perception nor an external object susceptible to sensation, present perception would not be useful. A concept is not something whose meaning could be confirmed by my personal remembrance of it, so it would not appear to be beneficial to focus much on memory in this analysis, either. Faith would only be appropriately utilized if the other forms of confirmation were to fail to substantiate the truth or falsity of the statement being considered. Finally, what a concept now is would not be affected by what I might intend for it to be; and I would not be able to affect the outcome in any event, because it is what it is. Thus, intention would be inapplicable in this effort, as well.

STEP 5. APPLY THE APPROPRIATE TYPES OF CONFIRMATION

a. External Authority

Because the form of assertion being considered is a definition, and because language is a socially developed tool, I will begin by considering the guidance that external authorities provide for the statement in question.

Definitions are simplified explanations of the meanings of words. We learn language, which is one of our primary mental tools, by means of explicit and ostensive definitions. With the former, we are told a specific meaning of a word; and with the latter, we are pointed to the meaning and have to figure the rest of it out from its context.

In spite of their relatively simple appearances, however, definitions can be difficult to formulate because language is an imperfect mechanism. One reason for this imperfection is that language, being a human invention, shares in human evolution and development, and, thus, it changes with the passage of time. As a result, no definition should be considered to be permanently fixed in all of its details. In addition, while definitions for our public languages depend upon social acceptance, society is never completely uniform, and variations among individuals and groups may cause the same word to be used in at least slightly different ways by different people.

But while definitions cannot be perfect, we need not try to make them so; for they can facilitate individual and interpersonal understanding and communication despite most imperfections. Our definitions provide us with indications of the commonly intended meanings of words which are generally accepted by credible sources. Of course, in order to remain generally accepted over time, they must be somewhat malleable; and in order to be accepted by diverse peoples and groups, they must be relatively broad and general. Neither of these features, however, is crippling, because the limited function of definition is to provide us with a certain minimal meaning which can then, if desired, be expanded as further analysis reveals more about the thing being defined. Definitions are-almost by definition-incomplete explanations, so a definition would fail only if it does not sufficiently indicate the generally accepted and commonly intended basic meanings of a given word.

Dictionaries contain lists of the current meanings of words as they have been discerned, formulated, and established by our linguistic authorities. They provide what most laymen recognize as the commonly intended meanings of all of the words set out in them. Thus, to begin with its most commonly accepted meanings, I looked up the word "truth" in a number of dictionaries.

My review of dictionary definitions of "truth" supports two general conclusions. First, reflecting that, as Alfred North Whitehead wrote, "In the realm of truth there are many mansions,"[1] the word "truth" is applied to a number of different concepts. Which concept is meant in any given statement depends, of course, on the context. Second, every concept can be defined in several ways, each of which would appear to be almost equally acceptable for most purposes. That is, there is more than one combination of words which can serve to indicate the same commonly intended meaning. These variations suggest that, around each distinct meaning, there are clusters of recognized definitions which deal with the same concept and that each one of them may be sufficient for most definitional purposes.

For the purpose of this treatise, I am not interested in all of the permissible meanings of the word "truth." The particular concept with which I am concerned has been defined in various dictionaries by the following group of meanings:

1. Being in accordance with fact or reality;
2. Conformity with fact;
3. Agreement with reality;
4. The state of the case;
5. The matter as it really is;
6. A true account; and
7. An established or verified fact.

All of these definitions derived from dictionaries are consistent with the various assertions propounded as parts of the correspondence theory of truth, as will become clearer below.

For purposes of convenience, I have referred to this concept as "factual truth." By focusing upon this cluster of meanings, I am excluding and not intending to consider the other alternative dictionary definitions of "truth" or of its adjective, "true," including faithfulness, reliability, honesty, virtuousness, legitimacy or "direction determined by poles of the earth's axis."

Another use of the word "truth" is sometimes accompanied by the capitalization of the word. When we seek the "Truth," we are usually not looking for factual truth but rather for an understanding of the universe and our place in it and, along the way, a comprehensive world view. In this sense of the word, we find potential answers among the religious and metaphysical systems of the world. But while the word "truth" may be of great significance to us when used in this context, I do not plan to address that usage any further, either, because the quest for "Truth" (which many times turns out to be more of a spiritual than an intellectual experience) does not focus on the general nature of factual truth or on how we may find it, but rather on different (and, from some perspectives, larger) metaphysical questions.

"Truth" is also commonly used in conjunction with different types of subject matter. We hear of "historical truths," for example, or "truths of aesthetics," "scientific truths" or "religious truths." Diverse as these subject matters may be, however, they are all concerned with factual truth-with truth as expressed ideas conforming to the facts in these fields. Even though aesthetic truths are generally more subjective and scientific truths are generally more objective, when we use and apply the word "truth" in this sense to different fields of endeavor, we mean essentially the same thing for all of them. For example, in aesthetic fields, we may say that "It is true that this painting is beautiful," and such an assertion is true if the painting is indeed beautiful. In a scientific endeavor, we may say, "It is true that this liquid weighs four grams," and the statement is true if we have something that is a liquid that weighs four grams. While the "fact" involved in the former is a position based upon aesthetics and in the latter is a scientific measurement of a wet mass that is subject to direct testing, both statements are true only if the specific things which have been described do in fact exist as they have been described. Thus, while this concept may be applied to different kinds of facts in diverse realms, it does so within the cluster of dictionary definitions described above.

Dictionaries are not the only external authorities on the meaning of words, however. To a considerable extent, they are passive and merely reflect uses of words by the general public at the time when each dictionary was written. In order to be thorough in this review and in order to try to be sure that nuances which may have been overlooked and changes which may be have occurred are taken into consideration, it is important to review other available explanations of the meanings of words. And the other major group of external authorities who should be consulted in this particular effort are the "experts" on the concept of truth-philosophers, of all ilks, kinds, makes and models.

The search for the correct description of the concept of truth has been a matter of extensive philosophical concern throughout much of recorded history. No single formulation has succeeded in becoming the final word on the matter, however, and none ever will, because we always need some flexibility in our definitions (of "truth" and of everything else) in order to be able to adapt them to different contexts and to changing needs. What has developed, however, over the history of philosophy (at least until the latter part of the twentieth century), is a primary way in which to answer the question of how "truth" should be defined. That answer is generally known and discussed as the correspondence theory of truth.

Under the correspondence theory, truth is considered to be relational: it describes the juxtaposition of mind and world, idea and thing, proposition and reality. In its traditional form, it holds that truth consists of "the agreement of knowledge with its object." An example of a more modern variation is that "The truth of a statement consists of its agreement with (or correspondence to) reality."[2]

The correspondence theory is characterized by the presence of three elements: (1) the mental assertion or statement, which says something about the world; (2) the thing that the mental element is describing or discussing in some way (an object or some other aspect of the world); and (3) the connector indicating the agreement or coincidence which occurs when the content of the mental element accurately describes or fits the thing being described.

The following is a sampling of various manners in which the correspondence theory has been expressed by philosophers over the millennia:

1. Plato: Statements "that say of the things that are that they are, are true, and those that say of the things that are that they are not, are false."[3]
2. Aristotle: "To say what is is not, or that what is not is, is false, while to say that what is is, or that what is not is not, is true."[4]
3. Anselm: "When what it affirms to exist does exist and when what it denies to exist does not exist, we have truth."[5]
4. Thomas Aquinas: Truth is found in "the adequation of thing and intellect."[6]
5. Spinoza: "A true idea must agree with that of which it is the idea."[7]
6. Descartes: "The word 'truth,' in the strict sense, denotes the conformity of thought with its object."[8]
7. Gottfried Leibniz: "Truth is correspondence of the proposition in the mind with the thing in question."[9]
8. Voltaire: "Humanly speaking, let us define truth, while waiting for a better definition, as a statement of the facts as they are."[10]
9. Jacob Fries: "Truth is a matter of correspondence between thought and object, but the object is not something transcendent; it is simply an immediate cognition. Truth is a relation between two levels of cognition."[11]
10. William James: "Truth is a property of certain of our ideas. It means their agreement, as falsity means their disagreement, with reality."[12]
11. Alfred North Whitehead: "Truth is the conformation of Appearance to Reality."[13]
12. George Santayana: "An opinion is true if what it is talking about is constituted as the opinion asserts it to be constituted. . . . It is a question of identity between a fact asserted and a fact existing."[14]
13. G. E. Moore: "To say that a belief is true is to say that the *fact to which it refers is* or has being; while to say that a belief is false is to say that the fact to which it refers is not–that there is no such fact."[15]
14. Bertrand Russell: "The world contains *facts* . . . and there are also *beliefs*, which have reference to facts, and by reference to facts are either true or false."[16]
15. Ludwig Wittgenstein: "The picture agrees with reality or not; it is right or wrong, true or false"[17]; and "What the picture represents is its sense. In the agreement or disagreement of its sense with reality, its truth or falsity consists."[18]
16. W. V. Quine: "Meaning matching fact equals truth."[19]
17. J. L. Mackie: "For a statement to be true is for things to be as they are stated to be."[20]

18. C. J. F. Williams: "To say that what Percy says is true is to say that things are as Percy says they are, i.e., For some p, both Percy says that p and p."[21]

These examples are part of a cluster of related definitions of factual truth from the perspective of a number of experts who have delved deeply into this subject. The variations among the formulations of these many basically acceptable ways in which the correspondence theory's definition can be stated demonstrate that there is no magic or perfect definition of truth, because almost every one of these formulations could be at least slightly reworded without significant damage. I also suspect that we could, for purposes of most philosophical discussions, agree to use the more generic examples of the correspondence theory, such as "A proposition is true if, and only if, it is the case," or "A statement is true if, and only if, the statement of fact it proposes agrees with reality." Which of the many correspondence definitions may be preferable in a given situation will depend at least in part upon the context of the discussion. Actually and in essence, it is not any particular formulation that matters here, but rather the distinguished lineage of this philosophical approach to factual truth that is most impressive.

While the correspondence theory has had a long and illustrious history, it has also been subjected to a number of serious criticisms. Consequently, these external authorities are nowhere near unanimity in their analysis of it. Most of its critics say that it is irrelevant, insufficient, incorrect, and/or meaningless, and they therefore contend either that other definitions or approaches, or that no definitions or approaches, should be used for the concept of truth.

The correspondence theory of truth has often been criticized as being irrelevant. This attack is generally leveled by those who believe truth to be something else entirely, to the exclusion of its factual sense. A quote from Nicholas Berdyaev demonstrates how these critics react to the correspondence theory:

> Truth is certainly not something in knowledge which corresponds to a reality that lies outside man. . . . Truth is God and God is Truth. . . .[22]

A number of theologians of various faiths have agreed that truth is God. Mahatma Gandhi turned the equation around for a while, saying that "God is truth"; later, however, he reversed himself and agreed that truth is God.[23] Arnold Toynbee, on the other hand, preferred the former order.[24] In Hinduism, truth is Brahman[25]; and in Buddhism, it is Nirvana.[26]

But truth has been associated with a number of other concepts as well. Marcel Eck said that truth is love.[27] For John Keats, "Beauty is truth, truth beauty."[28] Robert Browning wrote: "There is no truer truth obtainable/By

Man than comes of music."[29] According to Fyodor Dostoyevsky, truth depends upon our wills and is a matter of subjective personal freedom.[30] For Friedreich Nietzsche, "Truth is a woman"[31]; and "The very soul of truth," according to Vladimir Nabokov, "is the splendor of the creative imagination."[32]

The existential approach to truth also provides several alternatives to the correspondence theory. Miguel de Unamuno denied the "objective" or factual sense of truth and said that truth is subjectivity as manifested in authentic belief.[33] Along similar lines, Arnold Gehlen believed that our "inner certainties" are essentially irrational and "a reflection of the will on the intellect."[34] Indeed, except for the phenomenologists, many writers associated with existentialism have tended to eschew (or at least allege that they were eschewing) the factual concept of truth.

While each of these equations is interesting, and while some of them may even rise to the level of an acceptable alternative meaning of truth, they simply do not pertain to the concept of factual truth. Rather, they reflect efforts to emphasize the importance of their own diverse subjects. Those are legitimate efforts and inquiries, to be sure; but the perspectives of "truth" that they seek do not relate to factual truth or to the related dictionary definitions listed above, and they are thus beyond the scope of this treatise. A proper use of the word "truth" as "factual truth" still remains. We could invent a new word or words either for the concept of factual truth or for some of those other conceptions of it; but we should not need to go to that extreme, for different meanings of "truth" are simply not mutually exclusive. The factual concept of truth is highly relevant for all of us, no matter who we are or what we say. Therefore, the correspondence definition is not irrelevant and does not become invalidated simply because some of us may also be searching for other kinds of truth at the same time.

A second major criticism is that the correspondence theory is insufficient because it offers only an "incomplete" definition of truth. Those who have been dissatisfied with the correspondence definition on this ground have usually proceeded to explain exactly what it would take to make the definition "complete," and the two primary suggestions for that purpose assert the preeminence of the pragmatic or the coherence theories of truth.

William James, one of the more active proponents of pragmatism, believed that pragmatists accept correspondence as a basic definition of truth; but he said that pragmatists are distinguished by asking what difference it makes for something to be true:

> Ordinary epistemology contents itself with the vague statement that ideas must "correspond" or "agree"; the pragmatist insists on being more concrete, and asks what such "agreement" may mean in detail.[35]

Because of this position, most pragmatists would complete the definition of truth as "Ideas being in accordance with reality, as that correspondence is discovered and confirmed by the assertion's utility, success or stability."[36] Pragmatism has not generated long-term, widespread support as a separate theory of truth, however, primarily because of the difficulties in defining terms such as "usefulness" or "success."

The coherence adherents share with the pragmatists the same basic criticism of the correspondence theory-that it is incomplete. Brand Blanshard, for example, insisted that the correspondence theory cannot be definitional because it is not also criterial[37]—that is, it does not explain what criteria must be met before the "correspondence" can be said to exist. Nicholas Rescher said that correspondence is simply insufficient as a means of finding truth.[38] To provide a "complete" definition, these philosophers argue that the criterion for finding truth must be added; and they assert that the criterion for confirming a truth is its coherence with other known truths.[39]

One problem with this "incompleteness" criticism, however, is that the correspondence definition of truth is not intended to be criterial: it is merely aimed at describing what truth *is*. A basic definition is never a complete analysis; it is sufficient if it succeeds in conveying a correct indication of commonly intended meaning. To say that the definition of a door is "a swinging or sliding barrier by which entry is obtained" is neither contradicted nor invalidated merely by pointing out the many ways in which doors can be further described or how the mechanics of a door may be explained in more detail. Similarly, that there is more to factual truth than the correspondence definition should come neither as a surprise nor as a disappointment. We should not, however, discard an adequate basic definition on such grounds. Rather, we should build upon it with whatever knowledge appropriately adds to our understandings of the concept as we delve further into it.

Furthermore, we should not add to any definition of a word elements which are not commonly accepted even though they may be criterial or of other assistance. Going into such additional issues is unnecessary for a basic definition and would make it more cumbersome and less useful. For purposes of the basic definition of "truth," while criteria provided by both pragmatism and coherence are *among* the rational tests that can be applied in the confirmation of certain types of statements, neither of them has proved to be an exclusive criterion for all of our confirmations, because we verify truth by using a number of different means (including not only the rational) and a number of different tests within those means (including not only pragmatic or coherence tests but also others even within the rational means). Consequently, even if the definition of "truth"should refer to criteria for its confirmation, it would clearly need to include more than either or both of those two methods.

But then it would no longer be a basic definition which could be applied in all instances, and the additional properties or attributes would not always be needed or helpful, particularly when we want or need to employ only the basic sense of the word. Therefore, neither of them should be considered to be definitional for the word "truth," and the correspondence theory is not, as these proponents have alleged, insufficient.

A third type of criticism of the correspondence theory asserts that it is simply incorrect. One of the two major contentions challenging its correctness is that it is in error because we are not able to apprehend any object (or reality) as it *really* is. According to this argument, since we cannot directly know the objects or "things-in-themselves," we can never be sure that our assertions actually correspond to their objects. For this reason, they argue that the correspondence definition is invalid: words are words and not facts, and one of the two things being compared is thus "a shadow with no separate identity." Brand Blanshard summed up this criticism as follows:

> In order to know that experience corresponds to fact, we must be able to get at that fact, unadulterated with idea, and compare the two sides with each other.... But when we try to lay hold of (a fact), what we find in our hands is a judgment which is obviously not itself the indubitable fact we are seeking....[40]

There are several defects in this criticism, however. To begin with, we have very good reasons for believing that we do get at things outside of ourselves which may be represented as "facts." Most of these reasons are pragmatic and inductive, and we reach them as we observe the consequences of events which would not necessarily occur if we were dealing with mere thoughts or "shadows." I see what appears to be a pothole in what appears to be the road, and, when what appears to be my car appears to hit it, I sense a jolt. I see what appears to be a hammer headed for what appears to be my thumb, and my thumb hurts when the hammer appears to hit it. I have abdominal pain, and what appears to be a surgeon appears to say that I need to have my gall bladder removed; I wake up later with a scar, and, after healing, the abdominal pain has gone away. People who argue that the things to which our assertions refer are only "ideas" and not facts are simply not convincing due to the many thousands of experiences that we have had with consequences which have been consistent with things existing and occurring outside of ourselves.

Furthermore, we should keep in mind that when we are seeking truth, we are mainly after something that is not reality itself but rather is *about* reality. Assertions require assertors, and so truth requires a consciousness capable of making assertions. Because truth is an event of consciousness, it is an entirely mental phenomenon; and truth can never be independent of consciousness.

We should, therefore, not expect to completely get away from mind in an effort to reach "unadulterated facts" in finding truth no matter how we approach it. But what we are able to reach is sufficient factual content for purposes of comparison with our assertions. As Georg Lichtenberg noted, even if we had "no conception at all of the true nature of the outside world" and even if we did not know "whether things outside ourselves really exist and exist as we see them," that is a "completely meaningless" question; for "We are compelled by our nature . . . to express ourselves in such way that we speak of certain objects of our perception as being outside ourselves. . . ."[41] All we can know is the knowable, and truth works with the "facts" as we are able to know them. This concern may be something that we need to keep in mind when we consider the issue of certainty, similar to the limitations that should be recognized on our acceptance of causality for rational verification purposes; but it does not show that we cannot reach enough "fact" for purposes of using the correspondence concept of truth in a meaningful manner.

Furthermore, we would not need to reach "unadulterated fact" in order to use the correspondence definition in any event, because some of its variations adequately deal with the philosophical problems of perception and the apprehension of "things-in-themselves." For example, according to Ernst Haeckel, truth is the correspondence of assertions to the "knowable aspects of things."[42] This does not make "facts" (whatever they are) superfluous, as contended by some who propose an "identity theory" of truth, which asserts that if the two sides of an assertion are both "propositions," then there can be no correspondence with "facts." The reason no such identity occurs is that, if you accept the argument that all we can obtain as "facts" are still mental events, they nevertheless are quite different from the kinds of mental events we have when we make assertions about them. Even if, as Fries said, truth is "a relation between two levels of cognition,"[43] those two levels are completely distinguishable. The "facts" of the matter at hand are fixed by our apprehension of them, while our assertions about them are descriptions of those apprehensions. Consequently, an adjustment in the correspondence definition such as the one proposed by Haeckel (in which assertions must accurately describe "the knowable aspects of things") shows that it can be adapted to work in this context, thereby coopting the epistemological problem of the perception of ultimate reality. This particular criticism of the correspondence definition is, therefore, in error. While the debates about the extent of our ability to know the external world present a philosophical question that is important in its own right, they simply do not destroy the correspondence definition of truth.

A second major attack on the correctness of the correspondence theory is made by those who have concluded that the word "truth" is undefinable. If the word is undefinable, then the definition provided by the correspondence theory is not correct (as would be the case for all of the other definitions of factual truth, as well).

To maintain that "truth" is undefinable, however, it must be shown how and why that would be so. The main arguments along these lines contend that if none of our possible definitions of "truth" and "falsity" are effective for a specific kind of assertion, then that gap in the extension of those definitions also destroys their potential validity for all other types of assertions.

The purported limited effect which is at issue here does not derive, as might be expected, from the long-standing disputes over whether truth can be applied to normative statements. Some people contend that there are no normative "facts" and, therefore, that no correspondence could exist between an assertion and any real fact in that area. While the debate over whether "truth" should be applied to normative statements has not been consensually resolved, it has never been contended that because a definition of "truth" may be inapplicable to normative statements, it would also be inapplicable to all other kinds of sentences. Many people have taken the position that "truth" should not be applied to beauty, but no one has argued that this alleged "gap" in the applicability of truth means that truth should not be applied to scientific facts or to sense experience. But that is exactly the type of argument which must now be considered.

One of the originators of this line of thought was Alfred Tarski. Based upon his conclusion that truth is undefinable in our ordinary languages, he proposed that metalanguages (or languages about language) are needed in order to reach an understanding of truth, to the extent that we might be able to do so. Using mathematical analyses and inductive proofs, Tarski created a semantic approach to truth through set theory and symbols. Even then, however, he continued to believe that truth was essentially indefinable, focusing his attention for a definition in a metalanguage on "satisfaction," as in "a satisfies F if and only if there is a satisfaction relation S such that $S(a,F)$."[44]

While analyses provided through semantic and metalanguage approaches should be considered in their own right as alternatives to the correspondence definition of truth, they would not be the exclusive manner in which to deal with it if an adequate definition actually is obtainable in an ordinary language. Only if "truth" is undefinable in an ordinary language (like English) could the correspondence definition be incorrect on this basis.

The main reason why Tarski doubted the definability of "truth" in an ordinary language stemmed from the apparent failure of philosophers to be able to resolve the problems of The Liar's Paradox, thereby arguably identifying a group of sentences to which truth, as it is normally defined, is inapplicable. The Liar's Paradox has been around for several thousand years. It alleges that assertions like "This sentence is false" undermine all of our normal understandings of truth and falsity because they cannot be true without at the same time being false, and they cannot be false without being true.

Upon closer inspection, however, it becomes clear that The Liar's Paradox actually presents no such problem because it misapplies the concept of truth. When we assert the truth of a statement, we must provide a full statement whose truth is legitimately at issue. We can assert that "It is true that 'A is B,'" but we cannot correctly say only that "It is true that 'A'" (unless we are implicitly asserting, as philosophers often do, that 'A' is a complete sentence, which is not the case here). A sentence, in order to have truth potential, must assert something; and in order to do that it needs, at a minimum, a subject and a predicate. For example, we can look into the truth of "The wind blows," but we cannot look into the truth of "The wind" without either implying a verb or veering off into a different concept than factual truth. We thus cannot be forced to try to determine whether it is true that "The wind." "This sentence is false" fails to meet the requirement of presenting us with a statement with truth potential because we are not given enough information about what it is that is actually being contended. Note that it is *not* the case that the sentence which really needs to be considered for its truth or falsity is "This sentence is false"; rather, The Liar's Paradox asserts only that "This sentence" is false. But what is "This sentence"? It is a noun and an adjective without a verb. The first two words in The Liar's Paradox ("This sentence") do not constitute an assertion or anything else which may be true or false. The last two words ("is false") make it appear to be a normal sentence, but that is not the case. "This sentence" would need to be referenced to or expanded into a complete assertion in order to be considered for truth or falsity; and until that sentence is identified, we do not know what it is that is being alleged to be true or false. Consequently, while the words "This sentence is false" sound like they make sense, they do so no more than does "That answer is false." Without any idea about what the question is, we cannot determine whether "That answer is false" is either true or false. We simply must have more information about what "this sentence" really asserts in order to be able to ascertain whether it is true or false. Therefore, this first and most common formulation of The Liar's Paradox should not cause any despair about either the extension of the correspondence definition or the definability of "truth," and it certainly is not a sufficient reason to conclude that the only answer must lie in complex metalanguages.

The same analysis applies to the second common formulation of The Liar's Paradox, which is "I am lying." The reason this is not a true paradox is that it also is incomplete in the same way: we need to know what I am lying *about*, and this fragment does not tell us anything about that. "I am lying" is neither true nor false without more information, so it also fails to undermine all ordinary language analyses of truth for the same reasons that apply to the first version of it.

A third common form of The Liar's Paradox is found in the following two sentences, considered consecutively: "The next sentence is false," and "The previous sentence is true." Those who accept that this version is a paradox say that a consistent truth value cannot be assigned to those statements because, if the first statement is true, the second one cannot be true, and if the second statement is true, the first one cannot be true. The problem with this version of the Paradox, however, is that no reason exists for coupling both of these sentences together in order to consider their truth or falsity. The statement "The next sentence is false" is always independently true whenever it precedes a false statement, and the statement "The previous sentence is true" is always independently true whenever it follows a true statement. The two statements in this version of The Liar's Paradox should not be deemed to have *necessarily* co-joined positions, because both statements can and must be independently analyzed for their own truth. Because it is neither necessary nor appropriate to believe that these two sentences have to be considered together, this third version of The Liar's Paradox should not lead to the conclusion that ordinary language cannot handle truth, either.[45]

The fact that the impetus which led Tarski to pursue alternative approaches to truth was defective does not in any way dispose of the theories which were developed through those studies, however. If they provide a manner in which to define truth that would be better than the correspondence theory, then those efforts should be recognized and applauded. But the semantic approaches to truth of metalanguages do not, in my opinion, provide a more effective definition of truth. To begin with, Tarski's conclusion was that we should use "satisfaction" rather than "truth" when seeking formal correctness. Why, when pragmatists were generally being excoriated for using "satisfaction" as the criterion for truth, Tarski would believe that satisfaction would be an acceptable alternative to correspondence is difficult to understand. "Satisfaction" remains a highly subjective concept, varying with the speaker, and it is not only less definite but also less definable than "truth." Furthermore, in the end, we still need to know how and when we have found truth, and formal semantic analyses do not seem to be particularly applicable to our lives (or at least to the everyday parts of them). They simply do not appear to help us determine whether "It is true that the dog is barking" in a manner that is as useful as the correspondence approach to truth. Finally, the complex semantic approaches do not connect with the strongly accepted and intuitively held beliefs which we have in the concept of factual truth. Therefore, this criticism of the correspondence theory, based upon its alleged incorrectness due to the supposed undefinability of truth, fails.

The fourth major criticism of the correspondence theory argues that it is essentially meaningless. One philosopher who wrote along these lines was P. F. Strawson, who developed the "performative theory of truth." The performative theory contends that "truth" is a word which is primarily used as an affirmation to show our agreement with a statement. Thus, it is argued that when we say "The statement 'A is B' is true," we are not saying anything new about the proposition "A is B"; rather, we are merely indicating our endorsement of "A is B." Strawson wrote that saying something is true does not describe the statement or the facts; it is rather a matter of emphasis.[46]

In much the same way, "deflationism" and "minimalism" have relatively recently become popular philosophical approaches developed in support of similar positions on the nature of truth. Those espousing deflationism and minimalism suggest that saying a statement is true is redundant and/or meaningless. In other words, to say that "It is true that it is raining" just means "It is raining."[47] Deflationists deny that the word has any independent meaning as suggested by its common usage and by those who accept the correspondence theory of truth. Consequently, most of these proponents hold that there is no separate property in "truth" and, therefore, that there is nothing that supports any such substantive concept (cf., "There is no there, there"). They say that if there is a property, it is at most only a semantic or linguistic one. The deflationist/minimalist theories focus on the use of language-on the manner in which the word "truth" is utilized and on its intended effect when someone affirms that a statement is true. For them, "truth" only has meaning in our affirmation of sentences (cf., "Because I say so!").

Clearly an affirmation component is usually involved when we communicate our belief in the truth of a statement to someone else. Taking the position that when someone says, "It is true that 'X is Y,'" he or she is *only* affirming his or her position that "X is Y," is not correct, however, for several reasons. To begin with, when we make such statements, we are not always expressing a personal affirmation that they are true, even though it may look like that is what we are doing. While I am trying to convince *you* to believe the statement, I am not necessarily communicating that *I* really believe the statement. Sometimes we know that we do not have enough information to be as sure of a statement as we should be in order to correctly affirm its truth, but we nevertheless go ahead and affirm a statement about the alleged facts anyway. In such cases, when we say "It is true that 'X is Y,'" what we really mean is that "I want *you* to believe that 'X is Y' is true, regardless of whether it is really true and regardless of whether I am personally affirming it." We also sometimes fail to tell the truth. Therefore, it is not the case that whenever we say "'X is Y' is true" we are always just affirming it.

Much more importantly, however, the fact that we often employ the word "truth" as affirmation does not fully explain what we are doing when we attach that word to a given statement. Truth is not merely an affirmation, because it is also a conclusion, which is what allows us to be able to appropriately make the affirmation in the first place. When we are honestly asserting the truth of a particular statement, we do so because we believe that we have concluded that it accurately sets forth the facts which are described in it. Therefore, we affirm the truth of statements for a good reason separate and apart from our desire to communicate our affirmation of them to others.

Furthermore, other people will expect us to be using the concept of truth in conjunction with having made an effort to confirm that the statement is an accurate representation of the facts. The recipients of such affirmations will take it to mean that they can have some assurance that our assertions are correct and that we are not just saying things without any regard for their correlation to the facts (particularly when, for example, we say things like, "That truck is heading straight for us! It's really true!!!"). Despite the popularity of deflationism and minimalism among contemporary philosophers, virtually everyone else continues to believe that the factual sense of truth has an independent substantive meaning and that it can and should be employed in the manner described by the correspondence definitions. We assume that when someone says that a statement is true, she is asserting something about those facts for a good reason and not just commenting about her personal relationship to a particular statement or about her intentions for it. We affirm statements in this particular manner (by calling them "true") because we have concluded that they accurately describe the facts, in addition to wanting to express our affirmation of their accurate descriptions of the facts.

Perhaps some of the reaction against the factual concept of truth inevitably stems from its elevated status. Whenever we put something on a pedestal, at some point in time thereafter, we seem to want to pull it down. "Truth" is on a pedestal, as are "beauty," "honor," and some other high-concept words. To reduce the impulse to tear down higher-up things, we can consider and use lesser-status synonyms for those words, which in the case of "truth" include accuracy, correctness, and the state of being sure, definite, unmistaken, unerroneous, factual, actual, and/or unquestionable. Does anyone really want to take the position that it is meaningless to say that a statement may be accurate or inaccurate, or correct or incorrect, or that we cannot know the difference between them? Accuracy attaches to a particular kind of statements (those which are accurate), but it does not attach to other statements (those which are not accurate).

We all act as if there are accurate statements and as if there are inaccurate statements as they relate to facts. We also know that those assertions are accurate or inaccurate whether we happen to personally affirm them or not. Because that is the case, truth (in the sense of factual accuracy) remains a quality of an assertion which is present when it does correctly describe the facts whether I affirm it or not. Similarly, when I affirm as "true" an assertion which is false, my affirmance of that falsehood will not make it correct. We are all aware of having mistakenly "affirmed" some false statements and of having "disaffirmed" some true ones. Granted, we are affirming a proposition when we honestly say, for example, that "It is true that 'It is raining'"; but we are also saying something about the results of our investigations into the accuracy of that description of the facts (we should not ignore the issues of whether it is *really* raining and of whether we have confirmed that rain is coming down).

Most of those who propound deflationism and minimalism also argue that "truth" is not independently meaningful because it is not a "property" in any substantive sense. A property in this context would be a trait or attribute of something–a characteristic, feature, or quality of a thing–which, when we have a group of things, may be shared by all, some, or none of them.

Accurate statements can be differentiated from inaccurate ones. "The sun came up this morning" and "A cat is an animal" are accurate statements, and "The sun did not come up this morning" and "A cat is not an animal" are inaccurate statements. Accuracy is a characteristic or trait of statements which are correct because they comport to the facts that they describe. Accurate sentences are, therefore, meaningfully distinguished from inaccurate ones, which are those which are not correct because they do not comport to the facts they describe. Correctness is, thus, the property of a certain group of statements (those which accurately correspond to their underlying facts, which may also be referred to as those which are true), and another group of statements will not share in that property (those which are not substantively correct and, hence, which are not true). We add something important to our understanding about a statement when we say that it is substantively correct.

That truth is an important "property"-and that it is not merely a speech redundancy-can be shown by the fact that when we consider the various combinations of sets of true and untrue statements, we believe that the true statements share something in which the untrue statements do not share. For example, consider the four different combinations which can be made with two pairs of true and false propositions, which may be represented as follows: "'A is B' is true" when that is indeed correct, and "'A is C' is true" when that is not correct; and "'X is Y' is true" when that is correct, and "'X is Z' is true" when that is not correct. Any number of true and false statements may be employed here, such as "A bachelor is an unmarried man" and "A bachelor is an unmarried woman" (relative to current English language), and

"2 + 2 = 4" and "2 + 2 = 5" (relative to our standard mathematical system). The four possible combinations of these two sets of statements are then: (1) "'A is B' is true" when that is correct, and "'X is Y' is true" when that also is correct (e.g., "A bachelor is an unmarried man" and "2 + 2 = 4"); (2) "'A is B' is true" when that is correct, and "'X is Z' is true" when that is not correct (e.g., "A bachelor is an unmarried man" and "2 + 2 = 5"); (3) "'A is C' is true" when that is not correct and "'X is Y' is true" when that is correct (e.g., "A bachelor is an unmarried woman" and "2 + 2 = 4"); and (4) "'A is C' is true" when that is not correct, and "'X is Z' is true" when that is also not correct (e.g., "A bachelor is an unmarried woman" and "2 + 2 = 5"). While someone could "affirm" each of these four sets, the two statements contained in the first set clearly share something that is not shared by any of the other three combinations of those statements, and that shared characteristic or trait is their conformance with their respective facts. That is a property, and that is why truth is indeed the meaningful and substantive property of assertions which are correct and accurate statements of fact.[48]

The arguments of those who support deflationism and minimalism contain yet another flaw. When these critics of correspondence write books and articles about their theories, they contradict their own contentions about the meaninglessness of this concept of truth with every sentence they write. They are then not merely taking the position that they are expressing a subjective affirmation of something without having made any effort to determine whether it is correct. No deflationist or minimalist would agree that they are only affirming the statements which they are writing; rather, they must believe that their statements are accurate and correct and that opposing philosophical statements are inaccurate and incorrect because of the work they have done in trying to make sure that their statements do agree with the facts and that those of their opponents do not agree with the facts. Hence, when they write something like "Saying a statement is true does not say anything new about the statement," they are not merely "affirming" that statement; they are also contending that they have confirmed the statement and that it is accurate. Deflationists and minimalists therefore accept and use the concept of factual truth because they expressly or implicitly assert that the descriptions contained in their philosophical assertions are correct due to their supposedly accurate depictions of the facts about those concepts as they have best been able to confirm them. Consequently, they both utilize and apply the concept of truth in and throughout their writings, which would not exist as serious works of philosophy without the presence of this other aspect of truth. That deflationists and minimalists have operated in this manner, which is contradictory to their underlying argument, further undermines their stated position.

Deflationism and minimalism are actually not so much theories *of* truth but rather are more properly characterized as theories *about* truth-in this case, that there is no such thing, substantively speaking. The deflationist/minimalist theorists are correct that when people say, "It is true that 'A is B,'" they are usually trying to communicate an affirmation of that statement to others (whether they are doing so honestly or not). But they are wrong in dismissing the existence of the second level of meaning in the use of "truth." We normally are not merely repeating ourselves or trying to say "*P!*" more loudly when we say that a statement is true. Rather, we also mean to communicate that our level of confidence in the accuracy of the statement is very high because we have determined that there are good reasons to believe that it comports with the facts, unlike many other statements which we know are not accurate or which we suspect may not be accurate. It is, therefore, not the case that the assertion of the truth of a statement and the assertion of that statement without the use of the modifier "true" are one and the same thing, and it is the case that saying "P" and saying "'P' is true" are two different things because of these two levels of meanings. Consequently, when we affirm that a statement is true, it is no "mere" or redundant thing: rather, we are also asserting that a significant distinction exists between it and some other statements because of what we have been able to conclude about the accuracy of that particular assertion.

I suspect that critics of the correspondence theory have developed their arguments, at least in part, in response to the problems which we encounter due to the limits that exist on certainty and the obstacles which we regularly confront in the verification of truth. But truth itself does not become diminished or need to be disregarded because of these limitations, and it does not become a meaningless concept because of them, either. We simply do not need to abandon it because we cannot reach perfection when we try to use it. It is not the case that "Truth is not true" any more than it is the case that "Beauty is not beautiful"or that "Goodness is not good." Epistemological nihilism is, in fact, even less viable than ethical nihilism. While a number of philosophers in recent decades seem to have become enamored of the deflationist/minimalist approach, their enthusiasm can usually be traced either to linguists, who are naturally focused on the function of language and symbols, or to a few others who bear some kind of political ax which they wield in order to advance their personal causes.[49] No matter how hard they may try, however, they cannot live without the concept of factual correctness (also known as truth), and they cannot destroy it. Deflationists can tell us that truth is meaningless until they are blue in the face, but, despite that input, we will continue to use the concept because it comports to the facts dealing with the accuracy of our statements. Once again, we need to remember that "truth" has a number of accepted uses and that the existence of one acceptable use does not necessarily preclude the existence of another one. In this case, our understanding and use of the word "truth" as a matter of emphasis when we want to affirm certain statements that we make to others do not preclude the existence of the conventional sense of factual truth as described by and through the correspondence theory.

The correspondence theory of truth has historically provided the most widely accepted approach to the basic definition of the word "truth" in its factual context. As such, it has functioned as the common denominator of the "truth" which we seek in many aspects of our lives when we attempt to identify and describe those statements which accurately represent facts and to distinguish them from those which do not accurately represent the facts. In this section, however, the main question is the extent to which the truth of the correspondence theory is supported by external authority. The objective, as set out in the discourse theory of Jurgen Habermas, would be to find a consensus which would then be able to serve as the ultimate justification and recourse that can be obtained as we try to reconcile conflicting input from external authorities.[50] I believe that those who contest the accuracy of the correspondence definition are in error for the reasons I have just explained, and my personal conclusion is that factual truth is the attribute of an assertion which occurs when the thing (or event, object, or occurrence) which is being depicted by the assertion is accurately described by it, as this position has been well and accurately stated through the cluster of correspondence definitions set out above. Nevertheless, while dictionaries are credible sources for definitions and while the philosophers quoted in the list of correspondence definitions referenced above include many of the most esteemed thinkers in the history of the world, dissenters from its accuracy apparently hold substantial sway among the external authorities who are professional philosophers today. Consequently, it would be inappropriate to conclude that a consensus presently exists that would support the truth of the correspondence definition of truth among the most relevant external authorities.

b. Reason

While external authority may be the most important means to use in the confirmation of statements about concepts, we should also attempt to apply reason for any independent assistance that it may provide. In the course of the above analysis of the various criticisms of correspondence which have been advanced by external authorities, a number of the rational issues have already been discussed. Several additional matters along these lines, however, should also be reviewed regarding the confirmation of the statement, "It is true that the cluster of assertions which variously state the correspondence theory of truth do accurately indicate what truth–in its factual context-really is."

One set of these questions focuses on the antecedents of the statements under consideration. We should carefully review the meanings of the different words which are contained in these assertions because they are antecedent to–and make each statement conditioned upon-those meanings. "Facts," "assertions," and "agreement" must all be understood, as must the systemic preconditions for the observational conclusions which we draw in defining concepts. When we spend inordinate amounts of time thinking and writing about these topics, however (as have I in this one), the likelihood is that our understandings of the words, subjects, and precedents are at least adequate for the task.

In the attempt to confirm or disconfirm this assertion rationally, we may also employ a coherence test. To some extent, this has already been accomplished by looking at various dictionaries and reading many works of philosophers dealing with the correspondence theory. In my opinion, the correspondence theory coheres not only with our conceptions of truth but also with the broader epistemological conclusions of lexicographers and philosophers of many different traditions and beliefs, and it also does not appear to be in conflict in any meaningful way with other generally accepted truths in these areas. Once again, however, a significant group of contemporary philosophers would demur from this conclusion.

Finally, we can apply a pragmatic test: Is the correspondence definition "successful," and does it "work"? If we define "success" or "working" by whether the definition provides a generally effective basic explanation of what it is that we seek when we look for factual truth, the correspondence theory-as presented in the various characterizations of it set out above-would appears to me to pass this test, as well. When we want to accurately express what it is that we are trying to find and confirm when we are looking for factual truth (which is what "is successful" or "works" in this context), the correspondence theory definitions do that. Similarly, when we want to communicate to others what we believe that we have obtained in terms of the accuracy of a thought, in my opinion the definitions of the correspondence theory effectively meet that standard, as well.

c. Intuition

While we can appeal to intuition as an independent source of confirmation for assertions about concepts, and while some people may intuit the correspondence theory and, thus, have another reason for accepting it, I must confess that I have studied this topic so long that I am not sure that I would be able to distinguish any intuition that I may have had about it from all of the left-over and partially forgotten research which I am sure is ensconced somewhere in my mind. Nevertheless, to the extent that I have had personal intuitions about the factual sense of truth, they have supported my acceptance of the correspondence theory as the correct approach to the concept of factual truth. In addition, while it involves a form of confirmation by external authority, I would note that some others who have written about the correspondence theory have also referred to their own strong intuitions along the same lines.[51]

STEP 6. WEIGH THE EVIDENCE TO DETERMINE WHETHER THE ASSERTION HAS BEEN CONFIRMED.

In reviewing my analysis of the application of the forms of confirmation and weighing the evidence, I personally find it to be substantially supportive of the truth of the general cluster of assertions which fit under the correspondence umbrella. During that process, I have also explained why I have concluded that the other approaches to the definition of truth neither effectively undermine nor present any credible alternative to the correspondence theory. Seeing no good reason to change my views on these matters at this point, my conclusion is that the evidence in support of the truth of the definitions provided by the cluster of assertions which variously state the correspondence approach to factual truth is convincing and that the specific statement which I have been considering about that should be deemed to be confirmed.

STEP 7. DETERMINE THE DEGREE OF CERTAINTY TO ASCRIBE TO A CONFIRMED ASSERTION.

The cluster of correspondence definitions described above clearly does not have universal support, and they do not approach indubitability, either. Therefore, the level of assurance which has been attained through this truth-confirmation effort does not reach relative certainty: it is simply not tautological.

I could contend, however, that the assertion about the correspondence approach should properly be characterized as having reached the level of effective certainty; because, while additional support for it is quite conceivable and doubts about it are present (and indeed, vigorously expressed), in my opinion, the prospect of its disconfirmation appears to be so remote as to be quite unlikely. The concept of factual truth has been around for millennia, and it shows no signs of going away. Those who have tried to reject or undermine the correspondence theory have, I believe, not only failed to do so but also have failed to present a viable alternative to it. I would further suggest that the rejection of the factual concept of truth cannot be rationally maintained because of the inherent self-contradiction of that position, which becomes evident whenever any such assertion is fully made (e.g., "It is, in fact, correct to say that there is no concept of factual correctness").

Nevertheless, and even though the truth of an assertion is not directly dependent upon any general recognition of its truth, the level of discord which currently exists about this issue must impact the assessment of the degree of assurance which its confirmation has attained. Therefore, I reluctantly have to accept the fact that its level of certainty should now be deemed to have reached, at most, only one of the levels of probability. In our certainty assessments, we have to consider whether additional support for the truth of an assertion is conceivable. In this case, it clearly is, particularly among the most relevant authorities. For these reasons, I am presently unable to conclude that effective certainty has been reached for my conclusion about the accuracy of the correspondence definitions.

STEP 8. DRAW A CONCLUSION ABOUT THE TRUTH OF THE ASSERTION.

For purposes of finding and confirming truth in definitions which are not tautological, the level of effective certainty should be attained. Because the confirmation which I have made about the correspondence definition cannot at this time be said to have reached the highest level of assurance attainable for this type of assertion, I cannot, under the truth-confirmation process described above, presently conclude that it is true. Nevertheless, when we are asking, "What does it mean for a statement to be 'true'?", I believe that the analysis in this chapter provides the appropriate and accurate answer: "The cluster of assertions which variously state the correspondence theory of truth do accurately indicate what the definition of factual truth really is." I therefore believe that my presumption about and use of its definition in Part I of this book were justified. An assertion which is true is true regardless of whether we may or may not have confirmed it, and it is certainly my hope that, in this case, its truth will out.

STEP 9. KEEP AN OPEN MIND FOR FUTURE EVIDENCE THAT MAY LATER HAVE AN IMPACT ON THAT TRUTH CONCLUSION.

Having reached this point, given that no alternative definition appears to merit further investigation at this time, I am now ready for Step 9, when further evidence about this assertion may later impact my truth conclusion about it. I look forward to learning more about the concept of truth in the future.

NOTES

1. Alfred North Whitehead, *Adventures of Ideas* (New York: Macmillan, 1933), p. 314.
2. Rescher, *The Coherence Theory of Truth*, p. 5.
3. Plato, *Cratylus*, 385*b*2, C. D. C. Reeve, trans. (Indianapolis, IN: Hackett Publishing Co.,1988), p. 7.
4. Rescher, *The Coherence Theory of Truth*, p. 5.
5. Anselm of Canterbury, *Truth, Freedom, and Evil: Three Philosophical Dialogues*, Jasper Hopkins, et al., eds. (New York: Harper Torchbooks, 1967), p. 93.
6. Thomas Aquinas, *De Veritate*, q. 1, a. 1, *ad. Resp.*
7. Baruch de Spinoza, *Ethics*, Axiom 6, G. H. R. Parkinson, ed. and trans. (Oxford University Press, 2000), p. 76.
8. Rene Descartes, "Letter to Mersenne: 16 Oct. 1639," *The Philosophical Writings of Descartes*, vol. 3 (Cambridge University Press, 1991), pp. 138–140.
9. Rescher, *The Coherence Theory of Truth*, p. 5.
10. Voltaire, "The Philosophy of Common Sense," *Gateway to the Great Books*, vol. 10, p. 472.
11. Alexander P. D. Mourelatos, "Jacob Friedrich Fries," *The Encyclopedia of Philosophy*, vol. 3, p. 254.
12. James, *The Meaning of Truth*, p. vi.
13. Whitehead, *Adventures of Ideas*, p. 309.
14. Santayana, *Realms of Being*, p. 402.
15. G. E. Moore, *Some Main Problems of Philosophy* (London: George Allen & Unwin Ltd., 1955), p. 267.
16. Bertrand Russell, *Logic and Knowledge* (London: G. Allen & Unwin, 1966), p. 182.
17. Ludwig Wittgenstein, *Tractatus Logico-Philosophicus*, C. K. Ogden, trans. (Mineola, New York: Dover Publications, Inc., 1999), p. 39.
18. James C. Morrison, *Meaning and Truth in Wittgenstein's Tractatus* (The Hague: Mouton, 1954), p. 110.
19. Quine, *Philosophy of Logic*, p. 3.

20. Mackie, *Truth, Probability and Paradox*, p. 22.
21. C. J. F. Williams, *What Is Truth?* (Cambridge University Press, 1976), p. 2.
22. Berdyaev, *Truth and Revelation*, p. 26.
23. T. K. Mahadevan, ed., *Truth & Nonviolence: UNESCO Symposium on Gandhi's Humanism* (UNESCO, 1969), pp. 57–58.
24. Arnold J. Toynbee, *Experiences* (Oxford University Press, 1969), p. 146.
25. Radhakrishnan, *Indian Philosophy*, p. 507.
26. Mahadevan, *Truth & Nonviolence*, p. 61.
27. Marcel Eck, *Lies & Truth* (New York: Macmillan, 1970), p. 169.
28. John Keats, "Ode on a Grecian Urn," *The Complete Poetical Works of Keats* (Boston: Houghton Mifflin Co., 1899), p. 135.
29. Robert Browning, "With Charles Avison," *Parleyings with Certain People of Importance in Their Day* (London: Smith, Elder & Co., 1887), p. 201.
30. Edward Wasiolek, "Fyodor Mikhailovich Dostoyevsky," *The Encyclopedia of Philosophy*, vol. 2, p. 412.
31. Fritz Mendicus, *On Being Human: The Life of Truth and Its Realization*, Fritz Marti, trans. (New York: Frederick Unger Pub. Co., 1973), p. 57.
32. Hannah Green, "Mister Nabokov," *The New Yorker* (Feb. 17, 1977), p. 34.
33. Peter Koestenbaum, "Miguel de Unamuno y Jugo," *The Encyclopedia of Philosophy* (1967), vol. 8, p. 184.
34. Arnold Gehlen, *Man: His Nature and Place in the World*, Clare McMillan and Karl Pillener, trans. (New York: Columbia University Press, 1988), p. 299.
35. James, *The Meaning of Truth*, p. 191.
36. Nicholas Rescher, *Methodological Pragmatism* (New York University Press, 1977), pp. 57–58.
37. Blanshard, "The Coherence Theory of Truth," p. 36.
38. Rescher, *The Coherence Theory of Truth*, p. 8.
39. E.g., Walker, *The Coherence Theory of Truth*, p. 2.
40. Blanshard, "The Coherence Theory of Truth," p. 37.
41. Georg Henrik von Wright, "Georg Christoph Lichtenberg," *The Encyclopedia of Philosophy* (1967), vol. 4, p. 464. He wrote, "It is just as foolish as asking whether the color blue is really blue." Ibid.
42. Ernst Haeckel, *The Riddle of the Universe* (New York: Harper & Brothers Publications, 1900), p. 292.
43. Mourelatos, "Fries," p. 254.
44. Hodges, "Tarski's Truth Definitions."
45. Even if The Liar's Paradox presented a real problem for the extension of the correspondence definition, I doubt that many people would consider the lack of applicability of the correspondence theory to this group of riddles or word games to be any more debilitating than the arguable lack of its applicability to normative statements.
46. J. Kincade, "On the Performative Theory of Truth," *Mind*, vol. 67, No. 267, Jul.1958, pp. 394–398.
47. Paul Horwich, *From a Deflationary Point of View* (Oxford: Clarendon Press, 2004), p. 26.

48. Some have tried to add another roadblock to truth being considered a property by alleging that a property needs a common explanation rather than a common characteristic. The latter is the case, however; whether an individual characteristic or trait like intelligence is inherited or learned (which would be the "explanation"), it is still a characteristic or trait and thus a "property" in this sense.

49. See, e.g., a discussion of the motives of some who desire to be "free" from objective truth in their quests for certain "liberations" in Schmitt, *Truth: A Primer*, pp. 229–232.

50. Habermas, *Moral Consciousness and Communicative Action*. On the other hand, see Irving L. Janis, *Groupthink* (Boston: Houghton Mifflin, 1982).

51. See, e.g., Schmitt, *Truth: A Primer*, pp. 31–32.

Chapter Seven

Using the Concept of Truth

While we do not have consensus on the exact meaning of the word "truth," I believe that we all recognize that the concept of truth (or of correctness or accuracy, if the reader still shies away from that word) is (a) meaningful, (b) understandable, and (c) necessary. No matter what the most precise definition of "truth" may be, we use the concept of truth regularly and effectively in all facets of our lives. Actually, we do not really need to know its exact definition in order to use the concept any more than we would need the exact definitions of "good" or "should" in order to make most moral choices.

The real answer that we usually seek when we consider truth–and the main thing that we want to know–is not so much what it is precisely but rather how to assess assertions made by others about truth which may or may not be accurate, because we know that affirmations of "truth" can be flung around pretty carelessly. While the common definitions of the factual sense of the word, as they have been supported by the correspondence theory, provide a sufficient basic comprehension for its use, we need to remember that adequate definitions are just the beginning point. All of our understandings about the definition of the factual sense of truth would dangle before us fairly uselessly without further development, because we also need to know whether, when, and how we can determine a statement/fact correlation.

To effectively employ the concept of truth, we must build upon our definitional understandings by incorporating assessments of both confirmation and certainty, as those processes have been described in the previous chapters. When we use the word "truth" as correspondence between idea and fact, we are able to find it only when we have confirmed the accuracy of the idea to the requisite degree of certainty. Consequently, when we want to apply the concept of truth, we need to consider both of those issues in order to be in a position to determine whether a specific assertion in the form of "It is true that 'A is B'" is correct. Confirmation and certainty are thus criterial not for the definition of "truth" but rather for the identification of true assertions. They must be assessed before we can accurately declare the existence of truth in any given true statement, because that condition may be found only after we have been able to conclude that the statement has been confirmed to the highest degree of certainty which can be reached for that type of assertion.

Finding and confirming truth is facilitated when we apply as much as we can of the full range of knowledge and wisdom which exists about it. As it turns out, a number of the major philosophical developments in theories about truth would need to be incorporated into any comprehensive truth-confirmation framework, which I believe should include the following elements:

1. The correspondence theory supports the basic definition of the factual sense of truth which we use in our lives, which (stated one way) is that truth exists when an assertion about a fact agrees with the reality of that fact.
2. That basic definition is insufficient for purposes of utilizing the concept of truth, however.
3. In order for us to use the concept of truth well, its basic definition needs to be employed in conjunction with the criteria of confirmation and certainty, because truth becomes known to us when we effectively determine that an idea conforms to reality as best as we can ascertain that.
4. The verifiability principle of logical positivists, who contended that an understanding should be obtained of how the truth of an assertion might be confirmed or disconfirmed before its truth should be considered, appropriately emphasized the need to conduct explicit confirmations in our attempts to discern truth.
5. We are able to confirm the truth of assertions by using the seven different types of inferences which are available for this purpose. These are based upon present perception, memory, reason, intuition, external authority, faith, and intention.
6. Each of these different types of inferences can provide support for the confirmation or disconfirmation of at least some statements which are potentially true or false.
7. The "clear and distinct" test and the coherence and pragmatic theories of truth provide important rational tools which can be used in our attempts to verify an assertion.
8. We need to be very careful if we propose the truth of any assertion which is either strongly counterintuitive or contrary to the most informed human understandings we have about it. Without significant support for contrary

positions, our fundamental intuitions and the collective knowledge of humanity cannot often be effectively rejected.
9. The full truth-confirmation process involves a number of steps which deal with the different issues that need to be considered as we do this. The more carefully these steps are taken, the more likely it is that our conclusions about the truth or falsity of specific assertions will be accurate.
10. Different kinds of assertions which have truth potential may be distinguished from each other in a number of ways. For example, those which deal with events occurring at a specific point in time are different from those which deal with mathematics.
11. Some of the seven types of inferences are generally more productive than others in the confirmation of different kinds of assertions.
12. We often find multiple inferences in support of or in opposition to the confirmation of statements, from which we must try to conclude whether the assertion has been confirmed or disconfirmed or whether we are unable to draw either conclusion at that time.
13. Even when we have successfully confirmed a statement, different levels of assurance may be ascribed to that result, ranging from relative and effective certainty through two major kinds of probability.
14. Only a statement which has been confirmed to the level of the highest degree of certainty which can be obtained for that type of assertion should be called "true." Statements falling short of that verification standard should be described as being only "probably true" or "possibly true" unless they have been or clearly would be disconfirmed (in which case the possibility of truth for that statement would disappear).
15. The deflationist/minimalist theories of truth focus on one level of meaning contained in our communications when we say that a given statement is true, for we are affirming that we want the listeners to believe that statement.
16. When trying to discern whether others are making correct affirmations of truth, we need to consider several different issues, including whether they are honestly affirming it and whether they have properly confirmed it.
17. The affirmation which we make about a statement when we carefully and honestly assert that it is true expresses the highest degree of confidence that we can have in its accuracy, because we have concluded that we have effectively confirmed the existence of the idea/fact correlation as expressed in that statement.

True assertions are not limited to those which we have fully confirmed with the requisite degree of certainty, of course, because many more truths than that exist. None of us could ever be exposed to, let alone be in a position to analyze, all of the true statements which have been made in this world. And many of the assertions which do draw our attention will never be fully confirmed by us, either, because of a lack of time or interest or resources. But when we do have the time and interest and resources, we are able to use much of the thinking which has been developed about truth to help us reach the proper conclusions.

Truth is an important end, but it is perhaps an even more important means. Whenever we obtain assurance of truth, we are in a position to employ the result with confidence. And that, ultimately, is why factual truth acquired through the confirmation of the correspondence of idea and fact is critical for every thinking being. When we have it, we are more successfully able to take actions designed to reach our objectives, because we obtain them more frequently when our actions are based upon the surest possible knowledge that is available to us.

Accuracy in mental representations about the world greatly improves the chances not only of the survival but also of the flourishing of the thinker (no matter what the nature or level of the thinking being that is involved). Attempting to find and confirm true representations of fact is an inherent mental activity which would exist even if no one had ever sought to identify the concept underlying it and even if no one had ever tried to define the words which we now use when we discuss it. Nevertheless, successful efforts to better define "truth" and to improve our identification of the standards which may be employed in utilizing the concept of truth should increase our access to both true thoughts and their corresponding benefits.

Index

Absolute certainty, 50–62, 64
Anselm, St., 105
Aquinas, Thomas, 23, 105
Arcesilaus, 6
Aristotle, 3, 14, 49n56, 105
Assertions, types of, 70, 74–82, 93
Assurance, degrees of, 50, 59, 61–66, 94–95, 121–22, 128–29
Augustine, 14, 44
Averroes, 46

Bacon, Francis, 17, 73
Bacon, Roger, 73
Basic statements, 51–53, 60
Berdyaev, Nicholas, 44, 106
Bergson, Henri, 19, 55
Blanshard, Brand, 5, 16, 36, 45, 108–9
Boas, George, 46, 56
BonJour, Lawrence, 20
Bradley, F. H., 15–16, 61
Bridgman, P. W., 32–33
Browning, Robert, 106–7
Buddhism, 106

Carnap, Rudolf, 18
Causation, 6, 33, 39, 47n11
Certainty. *See* assurance, degrees of; effective certainty; relative certainty; probablilty

Chardin, Pierre Tielhard de, 16, 22, 44
Circular reasoning, 35, 37–38
Clear and distinct test, 15, 17, 22, 36, 87, 127
Coherence test of truth, 38, 40, 78–79, 85–87, 120
Coherence theory of truth, 15–17, 36–38, 107–8, 127
Confirmation: necessity of, 3–7; types of, 9, 46–47, 72–73
Consistency, 17, 30, 33, 37, 87
Correspondence theory of truth, 100–122, 126–27, 129
Croce, Bernedetto, 19–20

Deductive logic, 13–15, 17–18, 32–33, 35, 38, 60, 56–57
Deflationism, 20, 114–18, 128
Descartes, Rene, 5–6, 14, 54–55, 105
Dewey, John, 61
Diamond, Solomon, 40
Dilthey, Wilhelm, 34
Dostoyevsky, Fyodor, 107
Drury, Michael, 20
Durkheim, Emile, 42–43

Eck, Marcel, 106
Effective certainty, 63–64, 66, 68n26, 94–95, 121–22, 128

Empiricism, 15, 18, 40
Epicurus, 18
Erskine, John, 45
Existentialism, 107
External authority: as confirmation, 21–22; validity of, 42–44

Faith: as confirmation, 22–23; validity of, 44–45
First truths, 17, 50
Fries, Jacob, 105, 110

Galileo, 19
Gandhi, Mahatma, 105
Gehlen, Arnold, 107
Gladwell, Malcolm, 41
Godel's Theorem, 35, 57
Gordon, William, 20, 41

Habermas, Jurgen, 119
Haeckel, Ernst, 110
Hegel, Georg, 15–16
Hinduism, 34, 106
Humboldt, Wilhelm von, 34
Hume, David, 18, 20, 47n11
Huxley, T. H., 54

Indubitability, 14–15, 50–52, 54, 56, 59–62, 109, 121
Inductive logic, 17, 32, 56, 88
Infinite regress, 37–38
Intention: as confirmation, 23–24; validity of, 45–46
Intuition: as confirmation, 19–21; validity of, 41

James, William, 15–16, 23, 43–45, 54, 64, 66, 67n10, 105, 107
Johnson, Martin, 16, 41
Jonson, Ben, 4

Kant, Immanuel, 15, 34
Keats, John, 106

Kierkegaard, Soren, 23, 44
Korn, Alejandro, 41

Language, 6, 20, 30, 33–35, 40, 55, 57, 60, 62, 97, 101–2, 111–14, 118
Laplace, Pierre, 19
Law of noncontradiction, 14, 56
Laws of thought, 14
Leibniz, Gottfried, 15, 105
Lewis, C. I., 12, 18
Liar's Paradox, 111–13
Lichtenberg, Georg, 110, 124n4
Lincoln, Abraham, 57
Locke, John, 118
Logical positivism, 18, 39, 127

Mach, Ernst, 51–52
Mackie, J. L., 37, 106
Mao Tse Tung, 66n2
Mathematics, 56–57, 128
Memory: as confirmation, 12–13; validity of, 30–31
Minimalism, 114–18
Mivart, St. George Jackson, 3
Moore, G. E., 105
Mothe Le Vayer, Francois de La, 44
Mo Tzu, 16

Nabokov, Vladmir, 107
Nicholas of Cusa, 34–35
Nietzsche, Friedreich, 107
Normative assertions, 63, 74, 80–82, 100, 111

Obviousness, 5, 15, 35
Ortega y Gasset, 33

Parker, Francis, 32
Pascal, Blaise, 19, 50, 67n4
Peirce, C. S., 17, 33, 43, 61
Performative theory of truth, 114
Phenomenology, 20, 55, 107
Plato, 14, 105

Poincare, Henri, 20, 34, 67n14
Pollock, John, 30
Popper, Karl, 39, 53
Pragmatism, 15, 17, 31–33, 36, 38–39, 87, 107–9, 113, 120, 128
Present perception: as confirmation, 10–13; validity of, 27–30
Probability, 62, 64, 66, 67n25, 94, 122, 128
Pyrrho, 35, 56

Quine, W. V., 16, 31, 33, 105

Rationalism, 14–15, 18, 40
Rauche, G. A., 39
Reason: as confirmation, 13–19; validity of, 31–41. *See also* deductive logic and inductive logic
Reichenbach, Hans, 32, 39
Relative certainty, 62–64, 66, 94–95, 121
Rescher, Nicholas, 48n28, 108
Revelation, 22–23, 43, 57–58
Rogers, Arthur Kenon, 16, 35
Royce, Josiah, 32, 39
Russell, Bertrand, 18, 30, 36, 64, 105

Santayana, George, 37, 50, 105
Schmitt, Frederick, 20
Scientific method, 9, 18–19, 39–40, 63, 88–89
Self-evidence, 3–7, 31, 33

Sensation, 11, 23, 28–29, 51–54, 59–60, 63, 70, 77, 83–84, 95, 101
Sextus Empiricus, 35, 64
Siu, R. G. H., 9, 19–20
Socrates, 14
Sorokin, Pitirim, 9
Spinoza, Baruch de, 4, 15–16, 105
Stoics, 3
Strawson, P. F., 114
Systemic limitations, 62–63

Tarski, Alfred, 20, 111, 113
Toynbee, Arnold, 106
Truth, concept of, 99, 104, 106–7, 110, 112, 115, 117, 122–23
Truth, definition of, 1, 99–123, 127

Unamuno, Miguel de, 107
Uniformity of nature, 23, 33–34, 39, 56

Veatch, Henry B., 323
Verifiability principle, 18, 81, 127
Vico, Giambattista, 6
Voltaire, 105

Walton, Douglas, 42
Werkmeister, William, 32, 53, 57
Whitehead, Alfred North, 102, 105
Williams, C. J. F., 106
Wittgenstein, Ludwig, 31, 34, 105

Xenophanes, 50

www.ingramcontent.com/pod-product-compliance
Lightning Source LLC
Chambersburg PA
CBHW030116010526
44116CB00005B/275